The Living World of Faery

The Living World of Faery

R J Stewart

Illustrated by

Sarah Lever

GOTHIC IMAGE
PUBLICATIONS

Gothic Image Publications
7 High Street, Glastonbury,
Somerset BA6 9DP

Cover illustration Sarah Lever

Designed and typeset in Galliard by
Michael Mepham, Frome Somerset
Printed and bound in Great Britain by
Hillman Printers, Frome, Somerset

A catalogue record for this book is available
from the British Library

ISBN 0 906362 28 8

Contents

CONTENTS

CONTENTS

The Faery Folk

If my humanity I'd loose,
   Which seduction would I choose?
   The angels' voice eternal in the stars,
   Or faery folk, immortal mid the flowers?

The angels sing of boundless light and joy
   And spirit's flight to high rebirth,
   The faery folk are in the land
   And love the sacred earth.

R. J. Stewart. November 1992, written while
taking part in a day of sacred poetry
at St James' Church, Piccadilly, London

Acknowledgements

Personal acknowledgement must be made to the many explorers of the faery realm, human and otherwise, who have worked with me in Britain, Ireland, and the USA in recent years. Particular thanks to David Spangler for his deep interest in, and illuminating discussions upon, the contemporary development of the faery and Underworld tradition. Also to my partner Josephine, a seventh daughter, who took many of the contacts and ideas into areas that I had neither seen nor foreseen.

Some of the exercises in this book first appeared in different form in *Earth Light* and *Power within the Land* both published by Element Books, and are adapted here by permission. Extracts from an 18th century account in my possession have been slightly edited to simplify the language. My stories *The Song of Smallness* and *The Faery Harp* first appeared in *Magical Tales* published by Aquarian Press. Other stories, quotes, or adapted extracts are from classic sources, and are acknowledged as they appear in the main text. The cover and illustrations are by Sarah Lever.

R. J. Stewart, Bath, 1994

Author's message to the Reader

This is not a book on occultism or spiritualism. If you are familiar with my other books you will know that I regard occultism as being morbid and outdated, the product of repression in the 19th century. Spiritualists have claimed the faery realm, but have never been involved in the old traditions of faery that predate spiritualism by many centuries. The faery tradition is poetic and visionary, not dictated by spirits, but inspiring our own inherent spiritual vision.

You will find several sections in this book that talk poetically, of the legend of the Fall, and of Lucifer. These are not in the tone of religious propaganda, and there is no connection between the faery traditions of our grandparents and great grandparents and those of so-called "satanism". In folk tradition, the name "Lucifer" was attached to an old legend, similar to those myths of world religions that tell of the earliest ages, before human record. It is a legend of pre-human life in the planet, and how our planet is part of the stars, part of the universe.

When our ancestors were converted from paganism to Christianity, the legend of Lucifer and the Fall became part of the tradition, just as in ancient Greece the Titans fell into the Earth from the stars. The Titans were replaced by the Olympian deities, while Lucifer (the light of stars in the Earth) was absorbed into the Judaeo-Christian cycle of fall and redemption. Later we find the popularised identifications with evil, but they play no part in the faery tradition itself.

I could have used the word Phosphorus also from ancient sources, also meaning light within the Earth, just as the metal of the same name ignites spontaneously. But as my Gaelic and Welsh ancestors told tales about Lucifer and the hordes of angels and faeries, I felt that I should follow their traditional example.

R J STEWART, BATH, 1995

Foreword

The faery tradition is full of seeming paradoxes of time and place, of archetypical reality, the primal land and its inhabitants. It also reveals the difference between the ideal, and the incoherent and imbalanced, between realisations of that reality, that primal land, and its many inhabitants, human, faery, and otherwise.

The Living World of Faery offers many ways into the faery realm, including some methods of direct personal experience. It includes contemporary ideas and experiences, some being my own, some those of other people as I have learned about them and recorded them. It compares these modern experiences with older ones, for the faery tradition is very old indeed, and may be the oldest and most enduring spiritual and transformative tradition that we know. Religions rise and fall, societies, empires, and cultures come and go, as in Kipling's poem quoted on page xii, but faery lore endures in every country in the world. The faery races are timeless, as far as we are concerned, for they live according to a time pattern that we experience as immortal. This idea is explored in several of the later chapters.

Because the faery tradition was preserved and taught through tales and songs, there are several in this book. Some are my own, others are from the mainstream of faery tradition in Britain and Northern Europe. If you prefer to enter the faery realm through tales and songs, as your ancestors did, here they are. Indeed, you can, and should, regard this entire book as one rambling faery tale.

Far from being outdated, quaint or romantically obscure, the faery tradition is coming back. As an open secret, it has already had a huge revival. What is our greening concern with the environment but a 21st century restatement of the faery truth, taught by the old Gaelic seers, that all living creatures are interwoven, living upon and within one another? If some of the ideas and practices (old or new) found in this book are followed through with intent, in depth, they lead to a renewed conscious link with the land (wherever you may be), and with the living planet. As we move out of our isolated materialist antagonism towards our planetary environment, so we emerge into a new awareness where the best of science and religion, physics and metaphysics, finally come together. The foundation of all of these human endeavours at understanding, knowing, and relating to the world and worlds, is what is nowadays called the faery tradition.

Forget about little glitzy people in frocks, grow out of whimsical notions about cozy flower spirits and romantic back-to-naturism, for these are nothing to do with the living world of faery. It is not the world of fantasy, but of heightened shared reality. At present we use the old traditions to come to it, because they work. But the traditions themselves grow and change, and certainly are not limited to academic folklore. Soon we will come into that living world direct, and find that we have come home.

Introduction

Cities and Thrones and Powers

Cities and Thrones and Powers
    Stand in Times's eye,
    Almost as long as flowers,
    Which daily die:
    But, as new buds put forth
    To glad new men,
    Out of the spent and unconsidered Earth
    The Cities rise again.

This season's Daffodil,
    She never hears
    What change, what chance, what chill,
    Cut down last year's:
    But with bold countenance,
    And knowledge small,
    Esteems her seven day's continuance
    To be perpetual.

So Time that is o'er-kind
    To all that be,
    Ordains us e'en as blind,
    As bold as she:
    That in our very death,
    And burial sure,
    Shadow to shadow, well persuaded, saith,
    "See how our works endure!"

From *Puck of Pook's Hill* by Rudyard Kipling

The faery tradition is for everyone: it is the spiritual way of ordinary people, and was, and in many places still is, kept alive by the common folk of each land. So it is often a confused or confusing tradition at first, underpinning formal religion, surviving in oral lore rather than learned from books, containing elements from many sources. At its worst it can degenerate into ignorance and superstition. At its best it holds both the hidden relics and the foundations or sources of spiritual wisdom, ancestral lore, and of a way of communion between humans and other living creatures, both visible and invisible.

There is a tendency for some modern writers and revival pagans and New Age enthusiasts to sometimes invent a purely romantic fairy (not faery) tradition, with its origins in Victorian sentiment, spiritualism and Theosophy. There is another tendency running in parallel to the first, and with some links to it, which is to assume, without studying the tradition itself, that it is coherent, handed down intact through the ages, and that all we need to do is get back to it. Sadly much of this line of thought is wishful, similar to the grandiose claims of "high priestesses" in respect of modern magic or paganism. We shall return in several later chapters to the strong but widely misrepresented links between the faery tradition, varying ideas on witchcraft, and the future of spiritual paganism.

There is, despite the cautions mentioned, some historical indication that the traditions of faery and of seership were once formally and consciously upheld. Robert Kirk, writing in Scotland in the late 17th century (1), repeatedly asserts that "the old seers" as he called them, to make a distinction from those of his own time, had a complex philosophy with formal teachings, special training techniques, and held what we would today call a holistic worldview. Kirk may have been romanticising to a certain extent, for he was aware of the 16th and 17th century Rosicrucian texts, was widely read in the classics, and would have been drawn to the popular idea (dating back to the mythic traditions of ancient Greece) that each age devolved from the previous. Some of Kirk's descriptions of faery traditions and the Second Sight among his Gaelic parishioners are found in Chapter 13.

Amusingly we find Kirk's assertions about the old seers and the new repeated and embellished by the 20th century author Carlos Castenada, in the cultural context of one reputed branch of native American magic(2). Other features that are held in common are the Second Sight, working with otherworldly allies or companions, and the important idea of physical translation or movement between dimensions. All of these were described by Kirk some three centuries before they appeared in Castenada, but the traditions themselves are found worldwide, so there is no suggestion of blatant plagiarism in a literary sense.

INTRODUCTION

In both Kirk and Castenada we find the significant and practical idea that the folk traditions have a deeper initiatory level and that teachers and methods exist that are far more than superstition in practice. The ancient faery tradition, like that of Castaneda's 20th century sorcerers, is not a religion, but a way of relating.

In some of the later chapters we will find quotes from the work of American scholar W Y Evans Wentz, who as a student in the early 20th century compiled a thesis published as *The Fairy Faith in Celtic Countries*(3). As a field study this is still a classic, but it avoids altogether the initiatory and practical aspects of faery lore. Yet subsequently Evans-Wentz was moved to produce classic texts of Tibetan Buddhism for the West(4) which have strong magical and initiatory themes very close to those of the Celtic and Northern European faery lore, so his early thesis was not without a deeper effect upon him.

The faery tradition is not a faith, for faery beings exist whether or not we believe in them.

When we think of folk tradition and the oral continuum of faery lore, we should think of a loose but vast collection of ideas, themes, and practices, preserved in tales, songs, daily conversations and advice for ordinary living. Handed down through families and communities, such material has been found worldwide, with appropriate cultural and environmental variations. Modern scholars of folklore and anthropology have established academic systems of motifs (5) which often help us to sift and compare. Within this mass there were, and still are in Europe, genuine traditional wise men and women who realised and worked with deeper levels of the tradition. This has become confused with the claims of revivalists and New Agers, and it remains to be seen where the tradition will go, how it will transform itself. Some suggestions and conclusions are found throughout this book.

While rigid coherence and continuity of esoteric tradition is an escapist fantasy, another such fantasy is the currently popular idea of faery lore as "shamanism". In the last few years I have often heard it said, and seen in publication, that faery lore and Celtic tradition in general is "shamanic". Indeed, the word has become so fashionable that paying students can purchase accreditation in "shamanism" and "shamanic counselling". I often wonder how a Siberian wise man or woman, the true shamans still living and working today, would view this decadent nonsense.

In the broadest anthropological and mythic or magical comparisons, we find certain practices at a root level in every culture. So there are themes held in common between shamanism in the East, Celtic and faery magic in the West, Australian native wisdom in the South, and so forth. But there are also major cultural and environmental differences, for the shared properties of consciousness have to filter through the lands, the planetary zones, the peoples. Thus the faery tradition is about relating to life in the land, but it is not, and never has been, shamanism. Modern psychologised pseudo-shamanism has simply taken a few basic ideas out of their proper cultural context to promote them to needy Westerners. The commercial gurus of the 1960's and 70's did the same with Eastern religion, though they at least were drawing on material from their own culture.

The faery tradition is simply itself, a set of customs and practices preserved orally through the centuries in Western and Northern Europe. Moving further East through Europe and Russia toward Siberia, we find crossovers between this faery lore and true shamanic practices, but these are the same crossovers that are found worldwide when magical arts are traced geographically.

We could equally suggest that all shamans today are druids or sadhus or sufis or taisidhairs (the word that Kirk uses for seers). Thus we could have Celtic Sufism, Celtic Yoga, or Celtic Bhuddism, just as valid as so-called Celtic shamanism. The faery tradition is not exclusively Celtic, for it is also Norse, Germanic, Finnish, Lapp, Lithuanian and so forth. So we could propose Nordic shamanic sufism, or Lithuanian Buddhist druidism, with equal validity.

The entire silly discussion was clarified for me by two wise women, each within a genuine tradition (not New Age revivalists). One was an Australian aboriginal elder, while the other was a native American elder. In two separate hemispheres and continents they both said, quite independently of one another, that what they lived and worked with was not shamanism, it was simply and powerfully itself. I take my advice from these older and wiser women, and say the same of the faery tradition.

So What Are Faeries?

Faeries are living beings which are one step, one change of awareness, beyond humanity. They are also those which, out of the wide range of spiritual beings described in tradition, magic, religion and folklore, are most close to humanity. Once we make this change of awareness, our entire perception of other living creatures changes also. Usually the change is subtle, but it can be sudden and powerful. Some of the deep techniques of the ancient faery tradition, those undertaken by the seers and healers working with faery allies in folk tradition, bring such dynamic changes (6).

The relationship between faery and human beings is described in various ways in tradition or folklore, and has been encapsulated in various texts over the centuries. Such reports are consistent, we can see a close link between written accounts and the popular or folkloric beliefs still active and quite unconnected to the historic accounts (in the sense that they cannot have derived from them). When we look at these accounts, and at folklore from Britain and Europe in the 20th century, we find another consistent aspect: faeries in traditional accounts and beliefs are different from those in entertainment.

The commercialised images of little beings in gossamer dresses, mainly deriving from 19th century sentiment, are not part of the living faery tradition. When modern groups and individuals work with the tradition in terms of vision, contact, and inner transformation, they seldom meet Tinkerbells. Indeed, as reported later, many of the beings encountered are of human size or larger... sometimes much larger.

The theme of diminishing and trivialising is a reflection of something within the consciousness of Western culture, for it demonstrates our flight from, our rejection of, the subtle holism of living beings. It began with the propaganda of state religion, in which the older deities were decreed to be either evil or no longer valid. This theme permeated into folklore, particularly when country people were describing faery beings to churchmen or the upper classes. There is an ancient idea, found at least as far back as classical Greece, that the most powerful beings are intentionally trivialised, even mocked. This is well attested in Celtic tradition, in early texts describing the gods and goddesses in earthy mocking language. Later we find it in Gaelic superstition, where the "little people" are anything but little. Many cultures have this approach to names, nick-names, and initiatory or coming-of age names. The most obvious example is where huge powerfully built men are called "Tiny". This idea, where that which is powerful is intentionally called weak or little, has slowly become the entertainment fairy (not faery, which is a spelling used deliberately in this book to point out the difference).

Are Faeries Ancestors?

It seems certain that faery lore and ancestor lore are intertwined. So much so that in folk tradition it is often difficult to separate beliefs associated with ancestors, those connected to the dead and dying, and faery beliefs themselves. Many commentators, such as Lewis Spence(7) have argued that faery traditions are really those of an ancestral and death religion.

Others have observed that some of the magic and religion of ancient times have been preserved in faery lore and customs to the present day. This viewpoint often suggests that faeries are the remnant of beliefs in nature spirits, from ancient times. The New Age enthusiasm for faeries as nature spirits is not, therefore, new at all.

In the Underworld tradition, of which the faery tradition is a major branch, conscious work with ancestral consciousness is encouraged and developed. There are humans in the faery realm, according to tradition, who have chosen to be there (and some who are there by accident or through the designs of others). The most famous of these in Scotland is Thomas Rhymer, who is said to be the ambassador or mediator between humans and faeries. Another is the Reverend Robert Kirk, still active in the faery realm, into which he passed some three hundred years ago.

In this book we will deal less with the ancestral themes, though these are discussed at length in my books *Power within the Land* and *Earth Light* (6). Because of the complex connections of the Underworld, ancestral, and faery lore, both in tradition and in daily practice, you will find strands of all three themes interwoven in the following chapters, but with faery lore as the main emphasis.

Beings Large and Small

People are often surprised to find that far from being small and delicate, faery contacts are frequently large. There are several classes or types of faery being, ranging from those with a high level of individuality (often higher than that of humans) to those with a hive or collective nature. This interplay between individual and collective is found in human groups, families, tribes, and races also, and we need not pursue it further here.

What happens in actual experience is that while people are often expecting little butterfly people, or perhaps the Lordly Ones of the high faery tradition as expounded by W B Yeats (8) or Fiona Macleod (9) they meet something quite different. This is best demonstrated by some examples from actual encounters at group events and 'workshops'.

In a group working in England, one man was astonished to have a vision in which a faery being of huge size picked him up and carried him through a dangerous zone, as part of an exchange or agreement to help one another (the techniques for this type of inner work are described in Chapter 2. Prior to this he had been skeptical, thinking that trite little fantasy fairies would appear, and doubting that such beings were of any use as allies at all.

In Maine, USA, (March 1993) many workshop members described allies that were of huge stature and covered in hair, rather like the traditional Bigfoot. All expressed surprise at such beings appearing to them in meditation, and several were unwilling to talk about them at first, as they felt embarrassed by what they thought was a vision out of context. When other group members came out with the same experience, without any priming or hints or advance descriptions (as the forms are always left open to individual experience in workshops), this confirmed the encounter, and everyone discussed it more freely. This sharing of vision and encounters is a regular feature of modern group work: it is remarkably coherent without preconditioning or suggestion. Frequently a number of people will meet the same type of fairy being in a meditation or guided vision, or spontaneously see features, places, individuals, that are not described in the overall scenario.

In Manhattan (October 1992), most members of a workshop group, including myself, saw tall thin beings with distinctive eyes and high cheek bones. These are a classic type from the high faery tradition so beloved of "Celtic Twilight" poets and artists, though in this case they were naked, and not clad in the exotic armour, robes, jewellery that they would wear in Ireland. In this example, as in many others, the type of being encountered seems to relate to the land, to the locality. The group felt that they were meeting beings associated with the island of Manhattan, and with the sacred land, rather than with the modern city.

The unadorned style in Manhattan seems typically American: faery beings will appear naked, or clad in feathers, leaves, skins. The adorned style seems to be typically Scots or Irish: where the same classes of being (as those encountered in Manhattan) are dressed in scale armour, jewelled helmets, flowing robes of changing pattern and colour, ornately chased leather trews and jerkins, massive crystalline breast-plates, and so forth. One feature which occurs in both the USA and Britain, is that of intricate hair styles: hair in coronets, huge crests, flowing waves interwoven with colours and so forth.

Little Fairies

What about little fairies? Their appearance in folk tradition is usually taken for granted by modern people, but if we examine the actual beliefs, practices, ballads and tales of the faery lore, they are curiously absent. The little fairy is a literary or romantic extrapolation, perhaps an emasculation. It is the disempowering and fantasising of a living tradition that often involved powerful and terrifying encounters with beings of human type and size or greater. The development of the fantasy fairy in literature is well described by Katherine Briggs in her Dictionary of Fairies (10).

When we find accounts of little garden fairies, being the New Age wimps of the Otherworld, or the pederast fantasies of Victorian patriarchs, what is their relationship to the living tradition? The answer is: little or none. Having been ungenerous, we can let the pretty little creatures creep back a little into our imagination and consider their good points. At their best these little fantastical fairy concoctions, unconnected to the old faery traditions, encouraged some continuing belief in the otherworld. They are, of course, harmless. So they are comforting. The old tradition is not comforting, but disturbing and inspiring, transformative.

Some of the twee or cozy fairy fantasy is found in semi-serious presentation today. The idea of fairies as *devas* or nature spirits is perpetuated by the Findhorn community in Scotland, a successful New Age centre unrelated to the faery traditions of the land in which it developed. The Findhorn fairies (not faeries) are little people who make the plants grow, who teach about natural energies, and seem at best harmless. They certainly are not Scottish faeries, as can be demonstrated by comparing any Scottish faery lore to any accounts from Findhorn.

The basis for the Findhorn fairy ideas seems to be the Edwardian spiritualism of ROC (R Ogilvy-Crombey) who talked to nature spirits in the Botanic Gardens in Edinburgh, and made tapes describing his encounters which are still sold at Findhorn. Despite being a Scot, Roc's encounters are not in any way within the Scottish faery tradition in even the most remote sense of relationship. There is no reason to doubt his sincerity, or the reality of his experience, or its potential inspiration to others. But it is not a faery experience of the type described by Robert Kirk, or later by AE(11) or Yeats, or as documented in the extensive evidence of W Y Evans Wentz, all drawing from the lore of the Scottish and Irish people.

The beings described by Roc come instead from Theosophy, from Victorian and Edwardian spiritualism and fantasy, and (without being in any way disrespectful) from the genteel imagination of his generation, a fringe mysticism grounded in essentially harmless images and ideas which are easy to relate to, as they are mainly those of nursery entertainment. We need only to compare Roc's ideas of the god Pan to Pan in ancient Greek myth to find the difference, for whereas the first brings childish spiritual truisms, the second is a god inspiring joy and panic, older than the Olympians, master of all Nature, a mystery and a wonder.

The faery realm, you will be pleased to hear, is often humorous. In seminars and workshops I spend time on the differences between fantasy and tradition, though not as a preliminary to experience and contact, which must speak for themselves. During one group working, entering the faery realm, (see Chapter 2 for the method used on this occasion) I met with the Faery Queen in my vision. She is always beautiful and terrible, a spiritual being of great power. She held her closed hand out to me, and slowly opened it finger by finger. As she did so, a tiny winged fairy grew out of her palm. I was utterly confused, being certain that these fantasy creatures were not genuine. "Think again," she said, "we make these as specials".

I have spent some time with this important comparison, not to attack the ideas of the New Age or of Findhorn, which are appropriate for the people drawn to them, but to demonstrate the gulf between New Age ideas and the genuine tradition. That gulf has arisen through innocent ignorance and isolation, rather than through divisive intent.

If we are to live with the faery races and unite the separated and damaged worlds, we must first find out the true nature of our cousins. If you work with the ideas in this book, you will move towards such unity. How far you move is up to you, but remember that talking to flower faeries will not clean up Chernobyl ... but they might know someone of suitable stature who could help.

The Faery Experience

"I have never seen a man fairy nor a woman fairy, but my mother saw a troop of them. She herself and the other maidens of the townland were once out upon the summer sheiling (grazing). They were milking the cows, in the evening gloaming, when they observed a flock of fairies reeling and setting upon the green plain in front of the knoll. And, oh King! but it was they the fairies themselves that had the right to the dancing, and not the children of men! Bell-helmets of blue silk covered their heads, and garments of green satin covered their bodies, and sandals of yellow membrane covered their feet. Their heavy brown hair was streaming down their waist, and its lustre was of the fair golden sun of summer. Their skin was as white as the swan of the wave, and their voice was as melodious as the mavis of the wood, and they themselves were as beauteous of feature and as lithe of form as a picture, while their step was as light and stately and their minds as sportive as the little red hind of the hill. The damsel children of the sheiling-fold never saw sight but them, no never sight but them, never aught so beautiful.

'There is not a wave of prosperity upon the fairies of the knoll, no, not a wave. There is no growth nor increase, no death nor withering upon the fairies. Seed unfortunate they! They went away from the Paradise with the One of the Great Pride. When the Father commanded the doors closed down and up, the intermediate fairies had no alternative but to leap into the holes of the earth, where they are, and where they will be.'

"This is what I heard upon the knee of my beloved mother. Blessings be with her evermore!"

From *The Fairy Faith in Celtic Countries*,
W Y Evans Wentz, 1911

The Jackman's Song

The Faiery beame upon you,
The starres to glister on you;
A Moone of light
In the Noone of night,
Till the fire-Drake hath o're-gone you.
The Wheele of fortune guide you,
The boy with the Bow beside you,
Runne aye in the Way,
Till the bird of day,
And the luckyer lot betide you.

Ben Jonson

The Faery Song

How beautiful they are,
    The lordly ones,
    Who dwell in the hills,
    In the hollow hills.

They have faces like flowers,
    And their breath is wind
    That stirs amid the grasses
    Filled with white clover.

Their limbs are more white
    Than shafts of moonshine:
    They are more fleet
    Than the March wind.

They laugh and are glad
    And are terrible:
    When their lances shake
    Every green reed quivers.

How beautiful they are,
    How beautiful,
    The lordly ones
    In the hollow hills.
           From *The Immortal Hour* by Fiona Macleod

NOTE: The following extracts are from a substantial hand written book in my collection. I have modernised some of the English, and edited the extracts where they diverge into quotations from other sources. I hope to publish the entire account in the future. RJS

This is an account of my communion and confrontation with the People of Light, commonly known as Tripping Darlings, orfees or alfar, which is elves. Now the Rev Kirk, who went into their place in the last century, says that they do appear as a furious hardy host rushing at the seer from all Four Directions. This I would agree with, particularly at the onset of the seeing when they put us to the test. Yet he also says that they are of human appearance, and this is not always so. But as to those who say that the People are small and weak, they lie dismally, for even the smallest among the Host have powers more than those of a strong hearty man, while many of them are so great in stature that they defy our common sense and power of recognition. When the greatest of them knock upon your door you will not easily let them in, for some cannot cross the threshold as the dwelling will not accommodate them. Thus you must work to enlarge your abode and make its spaces clear.

Now as to the arguments of logical points I will defer to the learned Rev Kirk, who has assembled so many in his little treatise that I would be wasting labour to duplicate them, having a finely copied notebook of it on my shelf. But there are many details, fine and gross, that he has omitted to write, either from sensibility or the constrictions of the Church. Such details I shall record and present in this account to round out, give flesh to, and preserve certain aspects of our intercourse with these spiritual cousins or faeries. In time, after my own removal to that place which I earnestly desire to attain, this account also might be circulated among the brethren as that of Kirk is now. To this end I have set aside a small sum for a copyist.

There are many classes or orders of the People of Light, with their own habits, lives, structures of tribe family and the like. Some are well known to mortal men and women, others are invisible and hidden away, yet they will emerge at certain times or if bidden appropriately. It is mainly of these hidden orders that I shall treat here in detail, as those commonplace brownies, helpers, grain and cattle wards and well-keepers are widely known and still have intercourse with country people. Yet there is a more secret art by which the hidden orders are found and this shall be the core, the Pearl, of my account.

This art I learned at first in confused then clear dreams, as did the prophets and sibyls of old, but also from an aged woman cottager in Devonshire, and some Irish-Scottish seers in Virginia in the Colonies. Thereafter it is given to converse

and learn direct with the People in their own manner, according to their realm, element and hive or tribe. When Rev Kirk writes that women are not seers he is mistaken. I deem this not to be a lie, however, but a protection for the women of his own family, for he got the faery bloodline from his mother, as he tells us if we know how to read him.

By this deep art one may reach through pools, enter hills and trees, meld with stones, and come at last to the halls of the People of Light, who are within the body of the Land. And they may also come to you, for the threshold once opened may be crossed in either direction. You may see with their eyes and they likewise shall see with yours for mutual learning.

Extract from an early 18th century journal in the author's possession

Before exploring the basic elements of faery experience we should say that they have changed for modern people: the experience is different in many ways from that of our ancestors, different even from that of our grandparents or great grandparents in the early years of the 20th century. Although most modern entries into the faery realm and contemporary encounters with faery beings have some traditional basis, they are not confined within the framework of the old traditions.

Our published written and academic knowledge of the faery realm is found in folklore or in the older writers reporting the faery tradition before the development of formal folklore studies. All of this literary material, however fascinating and satisfying in terms of scholarly detective work and analysis, is the merest skin upon the surface of the faery and underworld traditions. More important than reports or studies is the oral lore itself, handed down through many generations, often with implications and subtle practices that were completely obscure to the scholars, collectors, and antiquarians. Such outsiders, often members of the privileged or upper classes and therefore isolated from old tribal or hereditary themes, came in to rural communities to note down the traditions, but they never lived them.

One of the few exceptions to this rule was Robert Kirk, a Gaelic speaker, and a seventh son (seventh sons and daughters are said to be especially gifted with faery powers). In 1990 I edited and commented upon his *Secret Commonwealth of Elves Fauns and Fairies*, a small book handwritten in the late 17th century(1). There are extracts from Kirk's remarkable book in Chapter 13.

Many family or tribal themes and arts within the old traditions have also changed... because we are working with a living tradition and not something fossilised in literature. Anything alive moves and changes.

The deeper levels of our modern faery experience remain similar to those deep levels of powerful magic reported in various ways through the centuries. They have slowly transformed from being integral parts of the profound religion and metaphysics of the pagan cultures into folklore and underground or secret initiatory arts. Even this organic change, however, is not the sole source of the differences between the contemporary and ancestral faery encounters.

The more immediate and dramatic forms of contact have changed during the last 50 years or so. This change becomes apparent when we compare traditional accounts, such as those given to W Y Evans-Wentz(3) in the early years of this century, with those of spontaneous or intentional contact in the period between the 1970's and the 1990's. Such changes are only due in part to the slow organic transformation of collective lore and imagination mentioned above, for there are other more dynamic forces at work which accelerate the process, and we shall return to this theme again in later chapters.

Differences Between Modern And Earlier Faery Experience

There are two significant major differences between the old oral traditional or ancestral faery contacts and those of contemporary humanity removed from oral tradition, and these two lead to many related minor differences. The first is that while our ancestors often sought to break away from the faery realm, many modern contacts are intentional. They are induced or encouraged by various means, ranging from naive New Age nuttiness to expansions and willed changes of awareness involving techniques handed down within the old traditions, but developed and applied in a modern way. We will return to this revision of the old methods in several places in this book. Not all experiences are willed, however, for some modern events are spontaneous, unexpected and unwanted, particularly those that seem to disrupt the comfortable conventions of materialism.

When the Reverend Robert Kirk wrote his *Secret Commonwealth* he stated that experience of the faery beings was a direct counter-proof to atheism and materialism, as faeries are our closest living orders or species of spiritual beings that extend through to ultimate Divinity. His thesis still holds true today, though we would probably propose it with a pan-religious and non-dogmatic emphasis, as Christianity is no longer a political or binding force in our culture. On a surface level we might say that dynamic encounters with faery beings prove that there is more to life than television, supermarkets, and computer games. On a deeper level we find that such interactions between the human and faery realm bring an undeniable knowledge of connection between all beings in our world.

Whereas Robert Kirk, a Scottish Episcopalian minister living at the dawn of the Age of Reason, was concerned with religion and atheism, we are concerned with the expansion of awareness in an imbalanced culture that threatens to destroy the planet. This brings us to the second and most important difference between the old faery experiences and the new.

The second significant difference is that whereas the traditional faery experiences were part of localised cultures relating to the land, modern experiences are both more individual and, simultaneously, on a greater and less regional scale. In other words the revival of our contact with the faery realm is an environmental and even global issue. This contact between human and non-human beings, once shunned and rejected, is now sought actively as a potential source of re-balance in a time of environmental crisis.

International Allies

The regional quality of faery allies is often commented upon, and has become a focus of attention in recent years, though in a rather diluted version, in New Age romanticism over faeries as nature spirits. The idea of spirits of place, or *genii locii* was widespread in the ancestral cultures, where deities often took localised and geomantic form, though such local forms were variants of the universal. In other words, while the power of the god or goddess remained the same, the locality modified its expression.

There were also lesser spirits of place, associated with springs, trees, hills, caves, landscape features, and the sacred sites attuned by humans. These comprise a large part, but not all, of what we call the faery tradition today. In England the faeries or place spirits are epitomised by Puck, often called Robin Goodfellow. In Kipling's *Puck of Pooks Hill*(12) Puck is a short broad brown fellow, who carries within him all the wisdom and power of the land. (This book is recommended reading if you wish to explore the English faery and ancestral tradition, of which it gives a very good sense). Robin Good-fellow, the other name for the same land spirit or faery being, is traditionally described as being a gigantic hairy man, who hides in the forest, but can help humans if they make contact(13). This class of faery being is sometimes encountered spontaneously in contemporary work, often by people who have no previous knowledge or description of them, and who may be expecting pretty little fairies.

So how do we relate to, and cope with, the old idea that faery allies may be active only in a specific locality? We live in a very mobile culture, and the idea of staying in one village for an entire lifetime is now becoming the exception rather than the rule. This attuning to the land is often felt to be a problem, particularly when we are working with the faery tradition in a variety of different areas, lands, and continents. How, for example, do my own allies, or those of anyone working actively with the tradition, relate to long distance or transatlantic travel?

In tradition we find what seem at first to be conflicting ideas. The old seers were said to lose their abilities when they travelled to America, and in Britain and Europe some wise women, men, and healers refused to move from one location on the grounds that their powers and allies would fail them if they did so. This idea, put forward in the 17th century, is simply one of many rationalisations of the experience of humanity attuned to a locality and a land, including the dialogue with faery allies generated by that land. My own experiences have been similar in many ways, though in the context of extensive travel.

In the late 1960's and early 1970's I was a pupil of the magician William G Gray(14), who practised a curious mixture of Kabbalistic high magic and more primal, even primitive practices, though this second level never appeared in any of his books. He told me on several occasions that when I developed my skills to a certain level the inner contacts (spirit, angel, or faery allies) would expect me to stay in one place. This working in one fixed location was what I did for some 14 years, but I do not do so now.

Yet there are also traditions of allies who move house with families, and some even get as far as other continents. In Katherine Briggs' *Dictionary of Fairies* (10) she lists examples of both American and Australian faery immigrants, connected to certain families. So while tradition teaches that faeries are linked to certain locations, and that our contact with them can fail when we leave these locations, there are faery beings that are free to travel, sometimes even emigrating.

To clarify this issue, we need to consider two themes. The first is essential throughout our approach to faery contacts: they are as varied, or more varied, than humans. Thus some, like us, cannot be forced to budge from home, while others are happy to travel. This commonsense approach should be applied to all faery and underworld contacts, and to spiritual contacts in general. The highways of contact can be crowded, and many into whom you bump are busy; some are friendly, some indifferent, some hostile. Just like a crowd anywhere.

The second theme is that of specific contact, connections, and alliances, and this is where we find deeper and more subtle ideas and arts coming into play. Faery beings vary in skill and power, just as we do, and folklore lists many types with quite specific functions. Some are linked to a house or locality, and never move from it. Others can and do move with families, though their function in the home or farm is, apparently, limited. Others are more subtly linked long-term (in our time sense) to a family or bloodline, and these are sometimes described as 'cousins'. They will appear to family members, and travel with them.

The more powerful the faery beings, the more flexible, mobile, and independent they are. Specific allies can and do travel great distances (as it seems to us), and are less confined to historic or tribal locations or to the energies of a specific place. In practical work we find that some allies and contacts work through a bloodline or family link, sometimes through tribe, clan or race (even though these distinctions are blurred nowadays), while other faery links are forged through intent.

My personal experience has changed with different phases of my life. As mentioned above, I had a long association with a powerful sacred site, and during that time found that a specific range of my abilities were reduced if I travelled, particularly when I travelled abroad. This reduction of power or awareness upon travelling is well known, and I have discussed this with several wise men and women within the native traditions of America and Australia. They too find that some allies and powers can travel, while others do not.

In the early 1980's my intense link with one power place suddenly freed itself. This used to be called the 'end of service'. In Scottish faery tradition Thomas Rhymer(15) serves the faery queen for seven years within the Eildon Hills (on the Scottish Borders). Once his time of service is over he emerges from the faery realm, which is for him found within one specific location under the hill. On emergence he is blessed, or perhaps cursed, with the power of the Tongue That Cannot Lie. Thereafter he utters prophecies, practices seershipseership, and so forth.

What we find in tradition and in individual experience is that attuning to a specific location can be a maturing or transforming process. Traditionally it works through multiples of seven years, just as the intensification of the Sight, of Healing, and of faery powers, comes to Seventh Sons and Daughters. In some people the attuning may become active in one location but they do not necessarily become free during one lifetime. In others it can accelerate into quite short and specific tasks at a variety of places. This variable phase usually comes in after the main period of attuning or service.

The oldest and most powerful level of service is found in the traditions of Sacred Kings and Sleepers(6). These are beings who are attuned to one location for long periods of time (in our time scale for thousands of years), sometimes as willing sacrifices. While Sacred Kings are originally human, Sleepers can be from various orders of life: human, faery, titan, deity or archangel.

After my own release from service, I found that I could travel more easily, and that many of my powers and allies travelled also. Furthermore I came into a new set of alliances which seemed to be extremely mobile. Some of these travel ahead, and in several instances make themselves known to people before I arrive. This phenomenon of advance contact has arisen on several courses or workshops in the USA, often with people who had no idea what they were experiencing.

Faery Work in Modern Groups or Workshops

I have used the rather clumsy word 'workshop' throughout, as it is well established now as a description of a gathering that is not a lecture, class, or seminar. At such gatherings people explore both the theoretical and practical aspects of a chosen subject, with a strong emphasis upon experience and acquiring certain basic skills and resources which enable them to pursue the subject further if they wish. There is also an emphasis upon mutual contribution of ideas, and sharing experiences, rather than a rigid teacher-pupil structure. This, at any rate, is how I would define a workshop, and how, in most cases, I try to pattern them.

I have been holding faery, underworld, and related workshops for about 12 years (from the early 1980's to the time of writing this in 1994) in Britain and the USA. The subject fascinates all kinds of people, from the hard-nosed sceptic to the open-minded. After all, we all heard fairy tales as children, but what can we do with the ideas in them as adults? The sceptic who expects to mock a vague cozy event about little beings with gauzy wings and frilly knickers will be surprised, for the approach is intensely practical and hard working, and most faeries are of human size or greater.

Equally surprised will be those who claim to work with 'devas' or nature spirits, as most of the popular New Age ideas along these lines have little or no connection to the ancient faery tradition of the Northern hemisphere. New Age fairies are instead based on a mixture of modern fantasy and Victorian sentiment, laced with the confused notions of the Theosophical Society which permeate many areas of New Age thought and publication. The approach in my own workshops, be they individual or group sessions, is not a purely psychological one in which the tales, images, and ideas associated with faeries are seen either as superstition or as expressions of sexuality and archetypical situations and relationships. In faery workshops we use traditional themes, images, and techniques to change individual and group awareness. We also enter (literally and in full awareness) the faery realm and encounter faery beings. In the more advanced stages of this type of work a dialogue is developed, a relationship in which the human and faery beings act as allies, and this alliance is gradually extended to other orders of living creatures.

This deep level of transformation of awareness is found in the primal spiritual traditions worldwide, usually among those rejected by political religions and preserved among 'uncivilised' peoples. Yet some world religions, such as Hinduism and Tibetan Buddhism, retain many practical aspects of such older traditions.

Beyond the level of mutual interaction and contact, is a deeper one again, which involves what is nowadays fashionably called 'planetary awareness', though this mode or quality of perception and understanding has long been taught in the old traditions.

So what happens in a workshop? Firstly no one is expected to believe anything: as a rule I find that believers are the most easily disturbed and disrupted by genuine faery encounters, as they tend to believe in ideas that are not found in the living tradition, and so have to unlearn some of the popular stereotypes about fairies, nature spirits, devas and so forth. This is similar to the difference between reading popular fantasy fiction about, say, Egypt,India, Tibet or the Antarctic, and actually going there. The romantic illusions are lost, and some people actually prefer to stay at home and fantasise.

Secondly, no one is analysed, psychologised, given advance clues or prepared: the entire workshop happens at face value and people are free to experience it without prejudice. Often the most materialistic or sceptical individuals have the clearest encounters, as they carry no imaginative luggage with them into the faery realm. For whatever we have in our imagination tends to appear in that place, sometimes to help us, and at other times as a burden to be cast away.

Romantic fairies are particularly unpopular in the faery realm. I suppose that they are the equivalent of television soap-opera, pop-video, or advertisement characters, the Kylie Minogues of the Otherworld. Naturally they pale into insignificance when we finally meet with real living intelligent beings.

The faery races are our natural allies between the outer realm of manifest nature and the inner realm of ever-becoming, of transformation, of boundless potential. They are our cousins in the art of perfection and health of the land and the planet. We have abandoned them and polluted the world, which means that we have abandoned and polluted ourselves, for the human and faery races mirror and complete one another. In the workshops I hold, simple methods are used to reopen our natural contact with these allies and co-walkers. All parties involved are then free to decide for themselves if they wish to take the contact further, and who are we to criticise those faery beings that do not accept or believe in contemporary humanity?

The Underworld Tree

The Testimony of a Lough Derg Seer

Neil Colton, seventy-three years old, who lives in Tamlach Townland, on the shores of Lough Derg, County Donegal, has a reputation for having seen the 'gentle folk', and so I called upon him. As we sat round his blazing turf fire, and in the midst of his family of three sturdy boys – for he married late in life – this is what he related:–

A Girl Recovered from Faerie.— 'One day, just before sunset in midsummer, and I a boy then, my brother and cousin and myself were gathering bilberries (whortleberries) up by the rocks at the back of here, when all at once we heard music. We hurried round the rocks, and there we were within a few hundred feet of six or eight of the *gentle folk*, and they dancing. When they saw us, and she struck my cousin across the face with what seemed to be a green rush. We ran for home as hard as we could, and when my cousin reached the house she fell dead. Father saddled a horse and went for Father Ryan. When Father Ryan arrived, he put a stole about his neck and began praying over my cousin and reading psalms and striking her with the stole; and in that way brought her back. He said if she had not caught hold of my brother, she would have been taken for ever.'

The 'Gentle Folk'.— 'The *gentle folk* are not earthly people; they are a people with a nature of their own. Even in the water there are men and women of the same character. Others have caves in the rocks, and in them rooms and apartments. These races were terribly plentiful a hundred years ago, and they'll come back again. My father lived two miles from here, where there were plenty of the *gentle folk*. In olden times they used to take young folks and keep them and draw all the life out of their bodies. Nobody could ever tell their nature exactly.'

Evidence from County Fermanagh

From James Summerville, eighty-eight years old, who lives in the country near Irvinestown, I heard much about the 'wee people' and about banshees, and then the following remarkable story concerning the 'good people':–

Travelling Clairvoyance through 'Fairy' Agency.— 'From near Ederney, County Fermanagh, about seventy years ago, a man whom I knew well was taken to America on Hallow Eve Night; and *they* (the *good people*) made him look down a chimney to see his own daughter cooking at a kitchen fire. Then they took him to another place in America, where he saw a friend he knew. The next morning he was at his own home here in Ireland.

'This man wrote a letter to his daughter to know if she was at the place and at the work on Hallow Eve Night, and she wrote back that she was. He was sure that it was the *good people* who had taken him to America and back in one night.'

From *The Fairy Faith in Celtic Countries*,
W Y Evans Wentz, 1911

On the 15th of October 17-- I went to the house of Elisabet Greening which was a small mud and wattle cottage on the edge of the village beyond the last house and before the marsh and woods. This hovel was quite overgrown with ivy, even to the rotten thatch of the roof. About it were some ancient trees, for it stood upon a low llys or dun mound where the trees had been before the house was built, and the garden was all thick with weeds and wild flowers, for she would allow no cutting or mending with steel in that place, though the villagers would have done so as a gift in return for her healing arts.

At my knock she opened and took from me immediately a small silver coin, which she bit and spat upon before dropping it into a large clay jar by the fire. Next she looked at me with one eye then with the other, putting her hand over one eye, right and left in turn. Her left eye seemed clouded or blind, but she said that she saw more clearly with that than with the right.

On the table she set a wooden bowl of water, and floated some straws upon it, and without delay bid me look into it if I would see as she did. At first I saw nothing more than the straws but she laid her hand over my head and the water swirled like a whirlpool and the straws spun around with it, dancing and glimmering. I pulled away for it made a pain in my eyes and a tearing.

Next, and again without preamble, the crone bid me rub some revolting salve upon the palms of my hands, the soles of my feet, my forehead, and in the hollow of my throat. I was loathe to take my boots off in that place what with the rotten filth of the floor but my desire for knowledge was strong. She later gave me the recipe for this salve which is hereafter:

Take a sealed glass such as is used for making flower oils from petals in sunlight. Into this put rose petals one pound weight, beeswax one half pound weight, and dried powdered wormwood broom-flowers, tansy, vervain and feverfew, a pinch of each. Clarify in the sun for three days or more if required, then add to the oily mixture the dried powdered caps of the red spotted mushroom about as much as will fill a large ladle amply but no more and no second ladle for fear you die of it. Leave the entire mess for three more days to blend its virtues. Now you strain the oily mix through pure washed linen that must be clean, until you have out the scented mass which you should do in the hottest sun so it will all run well. Use no fire to make it liquid, as this will corrupt its power. Now you throw the bulk and residue away where it will not be eaten by any animal or bird. You may bury it deep for safety in the midden or in the earth if you will.

Now you cover the oil, which should be golden brown with no flecks or particles within, with a black cloth as thick and dense as may be. Expose it only to the waxing moon each night until the moon is full. If there be any malefic aspects to your own horizon you may store it until the next full moon when they have passed if you prefer. At the full moon the oil will have thickened and you may mix this with a good goose grease, hog grease, or pure beeswax if you can get it with no particles. Mix it in the proportions one part of the oil to five parts of the grease, stirring well with a glass pestle but no metal. Keep the blended material out of the light in a stout air-tight box or jar.

As to the use you rub the smallest amount upon your palms, soles of feet, bosom, throat hollow, et pudendum et sacrorum secretum. Use no iron or steel utensils at any stage of this work and let there be no metal except perhaps copper in the storage jar if it needs hinging.

Extract from an early 18th century journal
in the author's possession

AUTHOR'S NOTE: Do not experiment with this recipe. It is not suitable for general use and may affect your health adversely.

In this Chapter, in Chapter Seven: *Diving through the Moon Pool*, and in Chapter Eight: *The Four Visions*, are a variety of techniques for gaining experience of the faery realm. I have used these in many gatherings with both beginners and experienced students, often with powerful results. If you do not wish to try these exercises, treat them as faery tales and read them through for entertainment. In all cases, the practical work is drawn from traditional material developed for modern use. In some cases it has been taught direct by faery allies, and is the means of contact for teachings such as those found in later chapters.

For those interested in the practical applications of the faery tradition, I would recommend, to begin with, even if you are familiar with this type of work, that you simply read these chapters as they appear in order in the book. If you are a beginner, try the basic exercises before you work with the longer visions. Read the entire book through like a novel or collection of stories before attempting any inner work. Having worked with the short basic exercises outlined, read the book again, and the links between the tales, visions, and discussions of traditional faery lore will become increasingly clear. Work with the longer visions by reading them through several times until you are familiar with their narratives, before you attempt them as deeper visions. There are guidelines for work in each example, and with practice you will be able to develop your own versions without using the text.

A Basic Underworld And Faery Realm Visualisation

The working visualisations used in this book are designed to establish specific contacts and generate broadly defined experiences within the Underworld and Fairy Realm. Many areas are left intentionally open, but the overall framework comes from tradition, reworked for modern use. If we reduce the many strands of such empowered visualisation to a very simple working, we have a basic pattern which may be worked in its own right, or into which specific images or intentions may be woven.

1   Begin with a short period of Silence, stilling Time, Space, and Motion.
2   Affirm and be aware of the Four Directions of East, South, West, and North. Then direct awareness Above, with the Moon, Sun, and Stars, and Below, with the Sacred Land and mysterious Underworld leading to the planetary heart of Being.
3   Begin by seeing the room or location or site where you begin with your eyes closed. See it with your inner vision, and be aware that the 7 Directions define it (i.e. ESWN, Above, Below, and Centre or Within). Visualise a circular closed door or hatchway in the floor before you. If

the working is done with a group, they sit in a circle and collectively visualise the closed doorway in the centre.

4 Open the door, with a clear affirmation of your intent to enter the Underworld and/ or Faery realm and seek the Light within the Earth. If you wish to reach a particular location, zone, or specific contact, define this now.(Some of these are described in later chapters).

5 See a steeply descending spiral stair, curving to the right. This stair is cut out of natural rock. Along the wall on the left hand side is a thick rope woven of red, black, and white strands, fixed into the rock by stone or bronze fastenings. Descend the stair.

6 The stair descends into a cave, chamber, or hollow within the earth. Sometimes this is a small underground temple. Usually you pass in through an archway under which a small lamp hangs, shedding a faint guiding light. In the chamber within, you pause in silent contemplation. At this stage various contacts may be made or visions experienced.

7 Return through the archway and ascend the stairs.

8 Climb out through the circular doorway, and close it behind you. See the doorway fade into the floor of the room in which you began your visualisation. It often helps to visualise the room or other location clearly (with the 7 Directions defining it), before you open your eyes.

9 Discuss if necessary, and take notes if you wish.

Notes: If you intend to work regularly with the Underworld and Faery tradition, you will find that simple note-taking can be helpful, but it should not be lengthy or obsessive. The most valuable things to note immediately on finishing a visualisation, either in private or at an outdoor site, are the following:

1 Any symbols upon the door or over the archway.

2 Describe the cave, chamber, or underground temple. It is usual to begin with a very simple rock chamber, but this often changes aspect into a related location. These spontaneous changes of location are important, and you may return to such a place at will. Your initial notes will help you to remember details for future visualisations, and for correlating dream work.

3 Describe any people, beings, or objects that appear within the cave or temple during your meditation. Objects that you are offered as gifts are particularly significant, as these are often keys to further working, and may be used in separate meditation upon their power and meaning, or as gifts that you tender at later stages of your work.

4 Describe the energies or power that you experience while in the Underworld or Faery realm, and how these affect you when you emerge from
the working.

Dreams

After empowered visualisation at power-locations or in private workings,
you may have unusual dreams. Any such dreams should be noted down, and
compared to the effects of your visualisations. Once again it is not necessary
to keep a bulky record or detailed notes, merely to be aware of any dreams
that you have involving Underworld or Faery images and powers, and to
compare these to your waking visualisations and visions. As a rule dream
encounters are not experienced in the defined imagery of visualisations, but
we are able to bridge between them and realise the connections. Meditation
on the links between dreams, defined visualisations, and spontaneous encounters form an important aspect of serious training in the faery tradition.
With time and practice, they will coalesce, but this can take several years.

The Inverted Tree Or Entering A Faery Hall

This more detailed vision uses some of the classic methods of entering the
faery realm and finding allies or co-walkers. It is designed as a group vision,
with one person reading or, with practice, improvising from the basic themes,
aloud. The rest of the group enter into the vision through the narrative.

It will also work powerfully for individual meditations, if you follow these
simple guidelines. To begin with, read it as a story. You might like to read
the longer tale *The Faery Harp* in conjunction with this, as it describes many
of the side effects of faery work, both positive and difficult. Once you are
familiar with the basics of this Tree vision, work through it a few times with
the book open on your lap. Next, work through with eyes closed, referring
to the book as little as possible. With practice you will find your own version
of this vision that you enter at will, without having to learn the full script.

The vision of the Inverted Tree is used in my Dreampower Tarot (16)
where the Three Realms of the Underworld (Stone, Pearl, and Whirlpool)
are accessed through a set of visionary trumps, radically different from those
in regular tarot decks. Indeed, it was from working with techniques such as
the one described next, that I was able to see and define the visions that later
became the Dreampower Tarot.

(Sacred Space is dedicated and opened. If working in a group, members
should sit in a circle. If two people are working, they sit opposite one another;

if three, in a triangular relationship; if four, in a square. The aim is always to visualise into the centre of a circle)

In the centre of the room we see a well in the floor. Build this image strongly: a circular well in the centre of the room, with a shallow rim. Now it becomes substantial as we look upon it, and we see that many fine roots are gripping the edge of the well, mingled deep into its fabric. These roots hold a fascination for us, and we long to look closely at them.

We rise and gather around the well, and one by one lean over and look within. The fine roots lead away into the depths below, lit by a blue-green light. We see that as they stretch away from us the roots thicken, leading into an indistinct brown shape that seems to float upon blue-green light below. At first the sight is blurred, as if something floats half-submerged in hazy waters.

Suddenly the image clarifies, and we realise that we are looking upon a tree. This tree is of such immense size that we could not register its image at first; it grows in reverse within the well, its roots around and within the rim, its crown far below. We follow the shape of the roots, leading our sight to a long brown and green trunk, leading deeper still to a huge spread of branches and leaves, far far below. The blue-green light is reflected up through the leaves from an unseen source in the depths. We look for some time upon this inverted tree, with its roots in our world, and its crown far below in the light. (*brief pause here for silent meditation*)

This is one of the trees of transformation, an inverted tree leading to another world. We know that if we wish to reach that world, we must climb the tree, from its roots to its crown, ever downwards. One by one we affirm our intent to travel the tree, and climb over the edge of the well.

At first the way is difficult, but as we progress, it becomes easier, with the widening roots supporting us as we descend. When we reach the wide platform where the roots emerge from the trunk, we pause and look below. The broad tree trunk stretches away beneath us, with immense branches growing out of it at intervals. This is the way that we must travel to the realm below. We see the branches spread out into an immense crown with shimmering silver and green leaves in constant motion, and below that a green blur of light that confuses our sight when we try to focus upon it.

Now we climb onto the trunk, and find that deep folds and grooves in the bark make movement possible, giving foot and hand holds before we reach the first great branches. One by one we climb onto the trunk, and feel the massive strength of the tree support us in our descent. Now we look up, and see for the first time that above us is a curious sky. It seethes with purple, blue and silver colours, with lines of light moving to and fro across it. Directly above our heads as we look up is a circular hole in the sky, with the roots of the tree disappearing into it. This hole is muddy brown and black, as if the roots penetrate into a circular bed of earth above.

Now we descend the trunk, and find that the way is increasingly easy. As we reach the great branches, a feeling of balance and lightness flows through us, as if we have left superfluous weight behind. Now we can see beyond the crown of branches, and realise that the green blur is a flat grassy plain far below. As we climb down, the branches and leaves gradually hide this plain from us, until we see nothing but the tree around us. Deeper into the crown we feel a crisp cool wind blowing around us, invigorating and exciting.

Now we are upon the slimmest branches, amid a vast cloud of rustling seething leaves glittering in the brilliant light. Suddenly we realise that the grassy plain is only a short jump away, and one by one we let go of the branches. We fall lightly to the ground, and as our feet touch it, we feel a thrill, a current of power flow through us for the briefest instant. We stand at the point where the branches of the tree barely touch the land below, and for a moment look up at the great crown and trunk leading far into the sky above, vanishing into a black hole. The sky has changed colour, and becomes blue and silver, emitting a sourceless light that illuminates the land brightly.

Now we turn and look across the plain. It stretches away, flat and green in all directions. The grass is full of tiny brilliant flowers, and constantly waves to and fro, sometimes with the direction of the wind, sometimes against it. We turn into the cool wind, and look out across the featureless plain: the steady flow of air makes our eyes water, and we turn our backs to the wind and look in the opposite direction. Far across the plain we see a mound. It seems to be a low grassy mound, with no distinguishing features.

We know that we must walk towards this mound, and one by one set out, with the wind at our backs.

As we move towards the mound our progress is fast; we find that we speed across the ground as if helped by the wind at our backs and the grassy earth beneath our feet. We are filled with deep power, as if every life energy within us is clarified, amplified, aroused. As we approach the mound we see that it is a huge grassy hill, long and smooth, featureless as if worn by wind and rain for thousands of years.

Now we reach the foot of the mound, and look up to its top. The grass and flowers flow over it without break or change, as if it has been folded up out of the plain without a break. Yet we know that we must enter into this mound, for our intent is to meet the People of the Sidh, the Fairy Dwellers in the Mound. The summit seems to flicker with a faint light from time to time, invisible if we look directly at it, yet clearly seen out of the corner of our eyes. There are no paths, no markers, and no sign of an entrance in the smooth grass wall before us.

Our intent is now to walk round the mound, and seek an entrance. We form this intent carefully, and one by one turn to the left, and begin our walk, following the shape of the mound, traversing its length. As we walk, the wind suddenly changes direction, and blows into our faces. It seems to resist our passage, but we steadily walk forward until we reach a state of balance between our motion and the wind in our faces. As we reach the far end of the long mound, the wind suddenly drops. In the stillness we hear a faint sound, like distant music, seeming to come from the ground beneath our feet. (*Short pause here*)

We make a turn to our right, around the side of the hill. Suddenly we come upon an entrance. It is a low stone box, made of two upright slabs roofed with a third massive capstone. It juts out of the turf before us, and we step round to look inside.

Within this small chamber we see someone sitting. This is the doorkeeper of the Fairy Mound, and for a few moments we look upon each other, beings from different worlds. (*Silent pause here*) If the journey is led actively, the doorkeeper may be described).

The doorkeeper signals that we should enter the chamber, which is very small. We have to bend, and immediately find that before us is a rough stone wall, with no further access to the hill. We look upon this wall, and as we do so, it begins to slide up into the earth above, revealing a glowing red light from within. There is a sense of urgency as it rises, and we quickly step through into the glow beyond.

As we enter the mound, the red light changes into a brilliant illumination of green, blue and white, and we find that we are standing upon a smooth stone floor inside the hill. Behind us the stone slab lowers, closing off the gateway. We are in the Fairy hall.

To our surprise, the chamber extends to our right and left, yet we entered by one end of the hill, and expected it to stretch away before us. We see a roof of natural stones tightly laid together and rising in a curve. Through these huge stones roots emerge; although there were no trees above the mound, the brilliant light comes from flaring torches in the roots, as if certain roots are alight. The stone floor of the chamber is marked with a complex interwoven pattern, rambling in all directions, seeming to elude sense, yet full of meaning and direction.

First we look to our left, and see there assembled a host of fairy beings. They are of many kinds and shapes, wearing costumes from many ages. Most are human in shape and dress, though many wear costumes of strange materials, while yet others are unlike any sort of being that we have seen before.

Now we look to our right, and see a great table at the far end of the hall. Behind this table are two tall thrones; one is made of rock and crystal, while the other is the huge stump of an ancient tree, still sprouting tiny branches and green shoots. Upon the rock throne sits the Fairy Queen, upon the tree throne sits the Fairy King.

We look first at the Queen: she has a white face and long flowing red and black hair. She wears a gown interlaced with veins of silver, gold, and crystal, and we see faint patterns bloom and move upon her face. Now we look upon the King: he has curling hair and beard, shot through with golden streaks. He wears a simple green tunic with a pattern of white flowers upon it, and his arms are bare. We approach the tables, and as we do so, we see the King and Queen in more detail. As we draw near to the Queen, the patterns upon her face seem to bloom and fade, like an interlacing of faint stems and leaves; her eyes are the fathomless eyes of a hawk. As we draw near to the King, we see that his hair and beard seem woven with glen wires or tendrils, and that his eyes are a deep green with black pupils. As we draw closer, we see their eyes change colour suddenly when they focus upon us.

Upon the great rough table of stone there is food and drink, cups and vessels. We are drawn to either the King or the Queen, and one by one we approach whichever of the two draws us. Now we commune with the King or with the Queen in silence. *(Silent contemplation and visualisation here)*

We are aware that the King and the Queen have exchanged something with each of us, and that we are bidden to turn and view the fairy hosts. Looking down the length of the great hall, with its burning root-torches and silver green light, we realise that out of the crowd certain beings have stepped forward. We are invited to choose companions from among those that come forward to us.

Look closely upon those that come forward as companions. You may choose one to be your partner, making a bond between the fairy world and our own. You need not choose whoever comes to you first, nor do you need to choose any partner at all. But you may only choose a partner from among those that come to you freely, and not from those that hold back. If you choose a fairy companion, choose carefully. If you do not choose a companion, be aware of your reasons for not choosing. *(Pause in silence here)*

Now we have chosen companions, or chosen to leave without companions. The size of our company has increased, and we know that it is time to leave the fairy hall. We walk towards the entrance stone, and when we reach it, hear the sound of wild music starting amid the fairy host. We long to stay, but know that we must leave. By the entrance stone we see the figure of a woman, in a long robe and deep hood. She holds a basket of woven reeds in one arm, and from it takes a gift for each of us as we reach the door. We cannot see her face, but we look closely upon the gift that she has given, and keep it safe.

Now the door stone slides upwards, and we step out into the tiny chamber beyond. There are three steps into the door chamber, and as we step through, the light behind us seems to turn red, and we hear the sound of shrill pipes and mellow harps. The stone slab slides shut behind us, and we see that the Doorkeeper is beckoning to us to hurry through the chamber and out into the land beyond.

As we emerge, we feel a strong wind blowing, with tiny drops of rain. It blows us back towards the tree. Looking into that direction we see only a spiralling column of smoke, faint and changeable, where the tree should be. There is a sense of urgency about our return to the tree, and we hear many creatures scurrying and running in the grass all around us, though we see nothing. We pass at great speed across the plain, and as we travel feel the quality of the light change.

As we draw near to the tree, it suddenly snaps into view, and we arrive suddenly at the point where its huge crown almost touches the grassy plain. The branches are whipped by the rising wind, and the leaves rustle and hiss loudly. From out of the heart of the leaves and branches two tall creatures step. They seem to be made of living branches, and each has a broad green leaf for a face. To each of us they come, one by one, and touch us upon the forehead.

With that touch we lose all sense of sound and for a moment experience the life of a tree or plant. We long to reach into the soil and up into the sky to the light, and experience a sense of time that is quite different from human time. (*Pause here*)

Gradually we become aware again of the wind blowing hard upon us, and know that we must return to the human world. We climb up into the branches of the tree, and begin our long ascent. The two tree-creatures have disappeared, but as we climb we are aware that our fairy companions and allies move with us, though have no sight of them. As we climb up the great tree trunk into the roots above, the land below blurs into a blue and green cloud, and we see above us a spiralling whirlpool of black and brown, into which the tree roots grow.

Now we approach that whirlpool, and it slowly ceases to spin, becoming a dark circular hole. On the other side of that hole there is a dim grey light, and one by one we climb through the well into a familiar room. At first it seems a shadow room in a grey dream, but we return to our original starting point, where we commenced our journey, and the room takes substance.

Now we look upon the well and the roots growing around it in the centre of the room, and it slowly fades, to be replaced by the solid floor. Our journey

to the Fairy realm is over, and we return to outer consciousness, realising that we have brought with us gifts and companions. (*Silent pause here*)
(*Notes are made, and if required people take it in turns to describe their experience. You do not have to describe your gifts or fairy companions if you feel that you should not do so*).

Freedoms and
Prohibitions

Crossing a Stream, and Fairies.— 'When out on a dark night, if pursued by fairies or ghosts one is considered quite safe if one can get over some stream. I remember coming home on a dark night with a boy companion and hearing a noise, and then after we had run to a stream and crossed it feeling quite safe.'

Fairy Preserves.— 'A heap of stones in a field should not be disturbed, though needed for building – especially if they are part of an ancient tumulus. The fairies are said to live inside the pile, and to move the stones would be most unfortunate. If a house happens to be built on a fairy preserve, or in a fairy track, the occupants will have no luck. Everything will go wrong. Their animals will die, their children fall sick, and no end of trouble will come on them. When the house happens to have been built in a fairy track, the doors on the front and back, or the windows if they are in the line of the track, cannot be kept closed at night, for the fairies must march through. Near Ballinrobe there is an old fort which is still the preserve of the fairies, and the land round it. The soil is very fine, and yet no one would dare to till it. Some time ago in laying out a new road the engineers determined to run it through the fort, but the people rose almost in rebellion, and the course had to be changed. The farmers wouldn't cut down a tree or bush growing on the hill or preserve for anything.'

Fairy Control over Crops.— 'Fairies are believed to control crops and their ripening. A field of turnips may promise well, and its owner will count on so many tons to the acre, but if when the crop is gathered it is found to be far short of the estimate, the explanation is that the fairies have extracted so much substance from it. The same thing is the case with corn.'

November Eve and Fairies.— 'On November Eve it is not right to gather or eat blackberries or sloes, nor after that time as long as they last. On November Eve the fairies pass over all such things and make them unfit to eat. If one dares to eat them afterwards one will have serious illness. We firmly believed this as boys, and I laugh now when I think how we used to gorge ourselves with berries on the last day of October, and then for weeks after pass by bushes full of the most luscious fruit, and with mouths watering for it couldn't eat it.'

Fairies as Flies.— 'There is an old abbey on the river, in County Mayo, and people say the fairies had a great battle near it, and that the slaughter was tremendous. At the time, the fairies appeared as swarms of flies coming from every direction to that spot. Some came from Knock Ma, and some from South Ireland, the opinion being that fairies can assume any form they like. The battle lasted a day and a night, and when it was over one could have filled baskets with the dead flies which floated down the river.'

Those who Return from Faerie.— 'Persons in a short trance-state of two or three days' duration are said to be away with the fairies enjoying a festival. The festival may be very material in its nature, or it may be purely spiritual. Sometimes one may thus go to Faerie for an hour or two; or one may remain there for seven, fourteen, or twenty-one years. The mind of a person coming out of Fairyland is usually a blank as to what has been seen and done there. Another idea is that the person knows well enough all about Fairyland, but is prevented from communicating the knowledge. A certain woman of whom I knew said she had forgotten all about her experiences in Faerie, but a friend who heard her objected, and said she did remember, and wouldn't tell. A man may remain awake at night to watch one who has been to Fairyland to see if that one holds communication with the fairies. Others say in such a case that the fairies know you are on the alert, and will not be discovered.'

From *The Fairy Faith in Celtic Countries*,
W Y Evans Wentz, 1911

Etain's Song

Enter Etain, in a coiled robe of pale green, with mistletoe intertwined in her long dark, unloosed hair. She comes slowly forward, and stands silent, looking at the moonshine on the water.

ETAIN: (*singing to a slow air...*)
Fair is the moonlight
And fair the wood,
But not so fair
As the place I come from.
Why did I leave it,
The beautiful country,
Where Death is only
A drifting Shadow?

O face of Love,
Of Dream and Longing,
There is sorrow upon me,
That I am here.

I will go back
To the Country of the Young,
And see again
The lances of the sidh
As they keep hosting
With laughing cries
In pale places
under the moon.

ETAIN turns, and walks slowly forward. She starts as she hears a peculiar cry from the wood...

From *The Immortal Hour* by Fiona Macleod

After sitting on a stool for the count of one hundred or thereabouts my eyes began to tremble and I saw twinkling lights flow through the air about my head. When I tried to blink the crone would shout at me to hold fast and strengthen my resolve, and suddenly she slapped me between the shoulders a resounding blow with the heel of her hand. Then the trembling passed and a mighty airy vigour filled me. Then a deep chill and shivering, then stillness and calm. Next the vigour returned but more fiery than before, rising upwards and causing me to gasp for breath. She told me to breathe deeply in a measured beat, and once the measure had been found by her slapping her hands upon the table, my body followed it without thought.

With the measured breathing the fiery vigour rose to my head and exploded in a burst of brilliant light and at that instant there was a ponderous knocking upon the cottage door so great and strong that the entire place throbbed like a bell. Elisabeth Greening bade me stand up like a man and open the door, berating me for my weakness. I was loathe to open it for I could not conceive what might be on the other side. Again she bid me open the door and suddenly cast the water and straws full into my face with a sweep of her hand. Whereupon I rose up, strode to the door before I could flinch and flung it open.

In the moonlight I could see a great bulky man tall and hairy leaning over me. With him and about him was a shimmering and a whispering, like a crowd in the distance yet close by. The great man placed his hands upon my shoulders, leaning down and over the threshold without crossing it with his feet. He blew hard into my mouth and filled my lungs and his breath was of fresh grass and sweet meadow flowers. I inflated with his air and my tongue began to mutter. Then he grabbed me around the waist, plucked me through the open doorway and strode off with me through the night.

We passed speedily through the village by a circuitous winding route snaking between the houses and not following the road. The stars began to stream over my head as he carried me out into the open now following a straight line without pause for hedge or stile and we ran full tilt into an oak tree. For an instant I thought myself dead but soon opened my eyes in a fair bright place swathed in luminousness and filled to bursting with a hosting of the People of Light.

Then certain burdens were laid upon me, some of which I shall recount in their proper place, some of which I may not tell lest I shatter the avowals of power that they embody.

I awoke on top of a grassy mound many miles from the village, at the foot of an oak tree. Far to the east I could see the outline of the hill where the crone lived, and used it to find my bearings. My new boots were gone.

Extract from an early 18th century journal

By looking at a general summary of prohibitions associated with faery contact, we can gain some valuable insights into the inner or energetic aspects of relationship between humans and faeries.

Prohibitions fall into three main categories:

1 Religious propaganda
2 Rules relating to disturbance of faeries and associated prohibitions connected to physical locations or areas of the land.
3 Prohibitions which may or should be broken intentionally to open out or close relationship with faery beings.

The 1st and 3rd groupings often interconnect, as the non-Christian faery traditions hold, even now, many initiatory and transformative aspects and techniques which the Church traditionally opposed. There are, however, a number of significant prohibitions in folklore which are not specifically based on Christian suppressive dogma, but are from within the faery tradition itself. These, within the third group, include eating faery food, using salve for gaining the Second Sight, calling faery Allies by name, exchanging gifts, vows, and making contracts.

Some of these can be used as powerful initiatory triggers, starting a process of change within ourselves, and we will return to them elsewhere, both in the general discussion and within some specific exercises for practical work. Before doing so we should look at the first two classes of prohibition in more detail, as each one has a number of subdivisions that give us insights into the relationship between human and faery races and realms.

1 Religious propaganda. This begins with the general ruling that any contact is forbidden, as it is supposed to put the soul at risk, as if the human soul is a possession to be fought over rather than an integral part of our individual and universal consciousness and being. Such sad rules are found in many religions worldwide, for organised religion often degenerates from an original pure spiritual impulse into something political, suppressive, and divisive. In the closely connected Christian, Jewish, and Islamic religions, communion with faery beings (equated in some ways with the idea of the djinn), with spirits, or with ancestral awareness, is frowned upon. Even communication with orthodox angels is regarded with some doubt through history, as it smacks of independent individual access to spiritual realisation. The underlying reason for disapproval is authoritarian, for orthodox religion seeks domination of the mind through fear of physical or spiritual punishment.

Overall the faery tradition is linked, at least as far as the historical attitude of Christianity is concerned, with the pre-Christian religions of the classical and Celtic civilisations, and with pagan culture and pagan traditions in general. The faery tradition in its broadest sense of enduring contact between the human and faery realms, the mutually-mirrored lands, predates and underpins many aspects of the formal pagan religions, and represents a deep strata of lore that has never been solely derived from any single formal religion, pantheon, or cult.

In Europe there is a general Christian prohibition against faery contact, but thereafter local and historical variants abound, as it is impossible in practice to prevent people talking to one another. Such people might be those of differing villages, regions, religions or races, or of other orders of life, or from other dimensions altogether. In daily life we find that ordinary folk had a dual attitude, for even the strictest chapel-going non-conformists or most devout Catholics would also leave food out for the faeries, experience the Second Sight, retain family traditions of healing and faery allies, and so forth.

Such complaints, prohibitions, and reports as we have from authoritarian sources, Church and State, often give insights into the practical faery tradition in earlier centuries. Caution should be the watchword with such reports, however, due to their extreme prejudice.

2   *Rules of Disturbance and 'taboos'* There are a wide range of negative rules associated with faery lore. They fall in sub-groups that are well defined in tradition, and which have some interesting associations for contemporary people, particularly in connection with earth energies and environmental themes. These earth energies are increasingly recognised in their own right today, though their long association with the faery tradition is not generally well known. Additionally, the earth energies are essential to that other aspect of faery lore, the initiatory and transformative techniques. These, which are discussed in (3) below and elsewhere in this book use earth or land energies as amplifying or catalysing sources for individual changes of energy and consciousness. We generally meet this idea in folk or faery lore as a set of disturbance 'taboos', rules that cause trouble if they are broken. The deeper lore, however, shows how these same forces, surrounded by prohibitions, ceremonies, protective charms, and superstitions, may be used positively.

The earth energy or land energy rules may be summarised as follows, bearing in mind that this is not a definitive list, and that many local and international variations are known:

a) Prohibitions against digging up or disturbing ancient sites, such as raths, mounds, tumulii, standing stones and so forth. Disturbance of mounds associated with faeries also merges with ancestral tradition and respect for the ancestral spirits. Folk memory accurately preserves the fact that the megalithic mounds in Europe are ancestral sites of religious or magical significance, but also states that they are the dwellings of the faery beings. Occupants of mounds can vary from humble earthy faeries, to the Lordly Ones of the high Celtic tradition, who merge with ancient deities, particularly in Irish legends.

b) Awakening Sleepers at ancient sites, either by accident or by intent.

c) Interfering with faery paths and lines, or cutting down faery bushes, trees, or flowers.

d) Moving, disturbing or destroying faery stones, which may be megalithic stones, cairns, or small seemingly innocuous stones.

Many ancient mounds were, of course, disturbed by treasure seekers, so the taboos against disturbance were not necessarily obeyed, even though dire results were predicted. Indeed, Kirk tells a typical tale of finding treasure in a faery mound, which has the sad conclusion that the starving women who found it, each inspired by dreams, traded it all away for oatmeal.

In Ulster, in 1991, I visited several megalithic sites, including chamber tombs and mounds. The remains of one such ancestral tomb were in the backyard of a modern farmhouse. When I arrived with friends, a young woman came out to greet us. At first she expressed amazement that we wanted to look at the stones (the mound that had once covered them was long since gone, leaving only the scattered stones of what had once been the inner chamber). Having realised that we were not agricultural inspectors or environmental activists, she gave us permission to go in. Before we went through her back garden she said: "There's supposed to be an old king buried there, you know, with a lot of treasure. Anyone who tries to dig it up loses the use of their arms and legs." Here was a modern woman telling a traditional story, rooted in both ancestral legend and historical reality, with a typical curse or warning attached.

Another contemporary tale, related to me by the author Caitlin Matthews, is that of the man who built an extension on his house, whereupon his three sons fell ill one by one. Two died, and the third was at death's door, when the father consulted a local woman reputed to be wise. She told him that the extension building had disrupted a faery line, and that he should pull it down. This he did, with his own hands, and his last remaining son recovered. This piece of modern folklore, connected to actual living people in a contemporary community, is something of a classic. Like the Ulster tale described above, it hinges upon the enduring idea which modern people still affirm, that certain locations should not be disturbed. In this second story the negative effect of disturbance is not dependent upon either belief or scepticism, and its cure is the destruction of a modern building. Both contemporary examples of faery lore hold ideas that have been in tradition for many centuries. While the first is significant of the tenacious endurance of beliefs, the second seems to involve actual forces at work that are a mystery to the participants.

Ancient burial sites, the subject of the first example, are often said to be guarded by faeries, to be the dwellings of faeries or ancestors, and generally held in respect. This could, conceivably, be a tradition handed down from the times when the ancestral sacred sites were part of the religion of a living culture, which is to say, from a time at least three thousand years ago, and perhaps much longer. Local traditions about mounds holding the remains of giants, kings, or heroes, are often borne out by modern archaeology. Providing we take folk memory as poetic rather than literal, it proves remarkably consistent and accurate.

The idea of faery paths and lines, found in our second modern anecdote, is somewhat different, and is so widely attested in tradition through the centuries that it needs separate appraisal. Whereas locii or power-sites are found as trees, natural stones, springs, hills, clumps of bushes, sacred sites and burial mounds, showing a crossover between the natural and the structured location, lines and paths are often 'invisible'. A faery line or path will cut across a field, or through a wood, often without linking two locations. There is a temptation for the modern mind to think that sacred sites, and ley lines reputedly connecting the sites, are another description of the faery locii and faery paths. This is not always so, and insufficient attention has been paid by ley-line researchers to the tradition of powerful faery lines associated with the landscape.

Though such lines may seem to go nowhere and link nothing, to disturb them is usually unhealthy. Within the faery tradition, of course, paths and lines that run from nowhere to nowhere are links between the realms, and are of greater significance than those between visible sites. Such faery paths are traditionally used in magical and initiatory arts for various purposes, including rapid movement from place to place, stepping through the realms and obviating physical distance in our own world.

In folklore we find this idea widely described in those reports of individuals who are seen to vanish at a certain spot and then reappear elsewhere, at some distance from the first location. A simpler version of this, often reported, is loss of orientation. In Cornwall it is called being 'pisky led', led in circles by the piskies or faeries. A typical example is that of someone who goes into a field but cannot find the way out, even though they (think they) know where the gate is.

The subject of land and faery energies is a major part of the tradition, and though much of it is a matter of experience rather than theory or rationalisation, some of the 'secret' rules are as follows:

To Find A Faery Line

Faery lines may be broadly described under two headings. First the ancient or enduring lines that are confirmed by local folklore, including 'secret' lines which are known traditionally to individuals or families. Second are those which are discovered either by accident or through intent. Ways of discovering such lines and paths are described below. This second group is by far the most widespread, and once you are attuned to the faery tradition you will be able to find such lines for yourself.

Most faery lines are semi-permanent, which is to say that you will be able to go back to them again and again, but they are not necessarily major landscape features. Other lines are of shorter life-span, arising for particular purposes, or through alignments of other contributing factors that generate a line, seeming to be spontaneous. Some lines recur over time cycles, so that you will find one on a certain day at a certain place, but it may not reappear for many years or even centuries.

Remember that faery lines and paths do not usually extend between specific geographic or surface points, so do not lead anywhere in the usual sense of connection. Some are very short, sometimes only a few feet or yards, while others will reach for miles. A faery line or path will vary in shape, straight, serpentine, or even circular, though closed circles are a different order or type of faery pattern. In some examples you may find lines that suddenly change direction, seeming to run straight then turning at a sharp angle of about 90 degrees. These are powerful lines that may be related to an overall pattern such as a circle or ellipse of features or other lines in the region.

Do not think of faery lines as part of a grid or overall energy pattern of the land: they may relate to such patterns in places where they exist, but they mainly emerge and extend between realms. They mark areas where boundaries may be opened out, and in some ways serve to dislocate and separate a literal topography rather than to connect it. So do not equate them with the popular idea of a grid of ley-lines connecting ancient sites, as this idea does not occur in the faery or Underworld tradition, and is mainly an invention of modern literature.

When Is A Line A Path?

In isolated rural districts you will find actual paths or slots in the surface of the land, often described as sheep tracks or old paths. Some of these may be faery paths. Other faery paths are found through following their linking features, rather than through any overt track, and this method will be described shortly. A faery line is where power flows over and through the land, but also flows between realms. You may be able to walk such a line, or you may be able to stand upon it and work with it.

While all faery paths are lines, not all lines are paths. This difference is important in practical work, as some lines are unhealthy to walk as paths, but beneficial to stand upon, meditate upon, and so forth. In many cases this problem does not arise, as the line flows into rocks, trees, up hills or over cliffs, and you would not usually expect to follow it physically. There are, however, powerful traditions where you walk into the rock, merge with the tree, run up the hill, and step over the cliff.

Think of lines and paths as alive, not circuits or conduits, but living connectives. They form a fluid palimpsest or organic network without any idea of a rigid overview or hierarchical map. This is a very important aspect of your understanding of faery power, rather like that of the hive nature of many of the faery races themselves. What seems externally to be a hierarchy or overview is in fact generated out of the fluid connections and mirroring of all parts within the whole. There is no grand plan of faery paths and lines, yet there is an organic whole, with connective factors that change ceaselessly. This point of view is similar to imagining complex solids or multidimensional shapes in geometry: each apparent view or map is only part of some other whole.

In the next chapter we will explore the idea of vows and contracts, which plays a major part in the faery and Underworld tradition. In many ways it relates to the third category of prohibitions referred to earlier, for the deeper levels of alliance in the faery tradition are found through breaking superficial prohibitions or taboos.

Vows, Contracts, Allies

Encounters with the 'Gentry',— When I was a young man I often used to go out in the mountains over there (pointing out of the window in their direction) to fish for trout, or to hunt; and it was in January on a cold, dry day while carrying my gun that I and a friend with me, as we were walking around Ben Bulbin, saw one of the gentry for the first time. I knew who it was, for I had heard the gentry described, ever since I could remember; and this one was dressed in blue with a head-dress adorned with what seemed to be frills. When he came up to us, he said to me in a sweet and silvery voice, "The seldomer you come to this mountain the better. A young lady here wants to take you away." Then he told us not to fire off our guns, because the gentry dislike being disturbed by the noise. And he seemed to be like a soldier of the gentry on guard. As we were leaving the mountains, he told us not to look back, and we didn't. Another time I was alone trout-fishing in nearly the same region when I heard a voice say, "It is – bare-footed and fishing.: Then there came a whistle like music and a noise like the beating of a drum, and soon one of the gentry came and talked with me for half an hour. He said, "Your mother will die in eleven months, and do not let her die unanointed." And she did die within eleven months. As he was going away he warned me, "You must be in the house before sunset. Do not delay! Do not delay! They can do nothing to you until I get back in the castle." As I found out afterwards, he was going to take me, but hesitated because he did not want to leave my mother alone. After these warnings I was always afraid to go to the mountains, but lately I have been told I could go if I took a friend with me.'

'Gentry' Protection.— 'The gentry have always befriended and protected me. I was drowned twice but for them. Once I was going to Durnish Island, a mile off the coast. The channel is very deep, and at the time there was a rough sea, with the tide running out, and I was almost lost. I shrieked and shouted, and finally got safe to the mainland. The day I talked with one of the gentry at the foot of the mountain when he was for taking me, he mentioned this, and said they were the ones who saved me from drowning then.'

'Gentry' Stations.— 'Especially in Ireland, the gentry live inside the mountains in beautiful castles; and there are a good many branches of them in other countries. Like armies, they have various stations and move from one to another. Some live in the Wicklow Mountains near Dublin.'

'Gentry' Control Over Human Affairs.— 'The gentry take a great interest in the affairs of men, and they always stand for justice and right. Any side they favour in our wars, that side wins. They favoured the

Boers, and the Boers did get their rights. They told me they favoured the Japanese and not the Russians, because the Russians are tyrants. Sometimes they fight among themselves. One of them once said, "I'd fight for a friend, or I'd fight for Ireland."'

The 'Gentry' Described.— In response to my wish, this description of the 'gentry' was given:- 'The folk are the grandest I have ever seen. They are far superior to us, and that is why they are called the gentry. They are not a working class, but a military-aristocratic class, tall and noble-appearing. They are a distinct race between our own and that of spirits, as they have told me. Their qualifications are tremendous. "We could cut off half the human race, but would not," they said, "for we are expecting salvation." And I knew a man three or four years ago whom they struck down with paralysis. Their sight is so penetrating that I think they could see through the earth. They have a silvery voice, quick and sweet. The music they play is most beautiful. They take the whole body and soul of young and intellectual people who are interesting, transmuting the body to a body like their own. I asked them once if they ever died, and they said, "No; we are always kept young." Once they take you and you taste food in their palace you cannot come back. You are changed to one of them, and live with them for ever. They are able to appear in different forms. One once appeared to me, and seemed only four feet high, and stoutly built. He said, "I am bigger than I appear to you now. We can make the old young, the big small, the small big." One of their women told all the secrets of my family. She said that my brother in Australia would travel much and suffer hardships, all of which came true; and foretold that my nephew, then about two years old, would become a great clergyman in America, and that is what he is now. Besides the gentry, who are a distinct class, there are bad spirits and ghosts. which are nothing like them. My mother once saw a leprechaun beside a bush hammering. He disappeared before she could get to him, but he also was unlike one of the gentry.'

From *The Fairy Faith in Celtic Countries*,
W Y Evans Wentz, 1911.

In the City

At the tea shop saw twinkling and then a host of the people sitting at disjointed angles among the regulars. Some were aping and mocking those more grave or pompous and when I laughed aloud the invisible guests all turned to me in surprise and then grimaced and stared and glared most violently for they had not known that they were observed. One wearing a tall red hat pursed his lips as if to whistle and blew at me until I felt the puff of his breath. In the midst of the tobacco and snuff fumes I caught a blast of cold damp water and dead wood.

Alas but my laughing next caught the attention of the mortals present and they too glowered at me until I regaled them with an utterly false reason for my mirth. When I had finished the tale all the mocking faery company had vanished from that place.

At an apothecary certain plants and compounds twinkled, while others, often the costliest, were dull and dead. Many of the metallic salts and remedies were chill and unwholesome even poisonous and destructive to health, while the plant based materia were good. I also discovered that by running my hand over the herbs that I could sense which were fresh, and this caused some disputes over purchases as the apothecary wished always to sell first those herbs that were old and weak, with all their virtue gone.

Extract from an early 18th century journal

As described at the beginning of the previous chapter, in the traditional faery tales and customs of Europe there are somewhat contradictory attitudes to making deals with faeries. The first is that of the Christian Churches, where contact is discouraged and conscious arrangements or exchanges are regarded as sinful and dangerous. The second, more widespread and ineradicable view and practice, was that of daily bargaining. This ranged from simple superstition, such as leaving out bread and milk (by far the most widespread) to carefully preserved hidden traditions among the seers and seeresses, the fairy healers, the workers of folk magic. These specific traditions, often well represented in faery tales, are the diffuse remnants of what was once a profound metaphysical tradition. We find traces of this in Celtic sources, and in classical literature on metaphysics and magic. We find it again in the Renaissance in Neo-Platonic philosophy and magic, and to a lesser extent in the magical revival of the 19th century.

Many of the confused or corrupt ideas on contracts and faery marriages are derived from the profound teaching of the Threefold Alliance(6). This fundamental idea in the faery and Underworld tradition (which is referred to in several of our later chapters) may be summarised as follows: humanity is incomplete. A complete being in our world is a balanced union between human, faery, and living creatures. From this tradition also comes the greatly trivialised idea of working with 'totem' animals and birds which has gained popularity in recent years.

The old seers and seeresses worked with faery allies for vision, knowledge at a distance, healing, and many deeper transformations and exchanges. Indeed, without the deeper interactions, the seemingly supernatural abilities cannot fully develop. They also worked with animals and birds, as allies, messengers, travelling eyes, sources of skill and power, and so forth. A threefold alliance of human, faery, and creature, can go anywhere in any realm or world, and is regarded as one of the major achievements of the faery and Underworld initiations. Yet it is only a beginning, for once it has taken form, the Alliance has to learn how to work together, and then undertake tasks.

Five reports of allies at work

To illustrate both the work of faery allies, and the ability of some allies to move great distances unhindered, here are three contemporary reports from the USA, and two from Britain. The first USA report concerns the popular identification of faeries with extraterrestrials, the next two are incidents in which a specific ally is seen by others in association with, or before the arrival of, the seer. The first report from Britain involves a specific ally appearing for the first time to someone not formally attuned to that ally, and was witnessed by a group of about fifty people. The second British report is a classic example of making a pact with a new ally, and shows how the Sight and making contacts often works.

1   A woman, who is a seventh daughter, told me how she looked out of her window one afternoon, and saw a shining spherical mass, with tall pale human-like beings emerging from, and returning into it, in large numbers. She ran for her video camera, but they could not be seen through the lens, only with both natural eyes. Nothing recorded on the tape, as she later discovered. She called her daughter to witness the event, and the daughter said "Aw, mom. Those're just space people. They're always hanging round here." After a short period of time, the beings vanished. When we compare this contemporary vision with that of AE, where many individuals emerge from a collective being, or with traditional descriptions of faery beings as tall, pale, and seen only with the second sight, we find a traditional context for the experience.

2   I arrived to give a talk in a bookstore in Greenwich, Connecticut. The lady who greeted me seemed very disturbed and unwilling to talk to me, which at first I could not understand. At the end of the evening she apologised, and said that she had been shocked to see a huge being walking in behind me. She was shocked not so much at seeing this ally, as she had had other visions in the past, but that she had seen it before. While working in the store on her own she had seen the same huge being examining the place, about a week before. This report interested me for several reasons: the lady had not read my books, and at that time those dealing with faery allies had not been published. She had no idea that I worked with a large ally (this is a type that traditionally works well with humans), and was clearly shocked, in front of witnesses, when I entered the store. The arrival of this being in advance was significant to me, as I had no idea that this was happening. She went on to describe two other beings that had 'checked out' the place before I arrived, and I recognised them both, but am not at liberty to describe them publicly.

3   While in Portland, Maine, for a workshop on the faery tradition I went to sign books in a nearby store. A woman who I had never met before, very agitated, asked me if she could talk to me. She said that she had had a dream in which a gigantic being had told her to come to the workshop, and that he was connected to me. This, being a dream, could have come from association, though once again, there was no way that the dreamer could know that one of my allies was of great size. It is only since contacts with this ally have been made by others that I have published any mention of it. As a rule the tradition teaches that you do not talk about

specific allies until others can tell you about them independently. Often the allies work in secret, and then will suddenly either vanish (as in the tale of the Six Servants) or make themselves more generally known.

4　While taking part in a joint event with John and Caitlin Matthews at Hawkwood College, in Stroud, England, the large group was working with a complex ceremony, meditation, and vision sequence that John and Caitlin had prepared. During the meditation, John was surprised to see, appearing from the South, behind his seat, a faery being in the form of a man-tree, like a wiry male with oak sprouting all over him. When asked who he was, this being said "I am Bob Stewart." John Matthews is an experienced seer, so he replied "No you are not. Bob Stewart is sitting over there on the opposite side of the hall." "Nevertheless" said the oak man, "I am he" and disappeared. None of this was in the specific context of the meditation.

When John described this to the group, he was mystified, and thought at first that the encounter was frivolous. But it was not frivolous, for by coincidence he was sitting between two of my students, who only a few days before had worked with me on the tradition of the sacred oak tree, and the beings associated with it. Each of them had been given a tiny dried twig from a very ancient oak tree, and put into touch with the oak-man contact, whom I have worked with for many years. This contact had been given to me by the late W G Gray, in 1970, and appears exactly as John Matthews described. Yet John had no idea that I worked with this being, or that the students next to him had just been introduced to the contact, which was often kept secret in the old tradition, and handed down through the generations.

What fascinated me was the way the communication worked:

a)　John did not know of the contact and was not expecting it.

b)　He was between two of my students, a man and a woman.

c)　The contact came from behind him, between the couple, moving through him to stand before him and speak. This is classic polarity magic, and is often used to link to faery allies in group work. But it was not the aim or intention of the event, it occurred spontaneously.

d)　The oak-man stated that he was me, and when challenged (an important aspect of the tradition is to challenge faery contacts if they seem to mislead you) he insisted that he was me even though I was physically present in another part of the room. In this way he made his link to me known, but also showed how such links are not limited by our conditioned ideas of 'separateness' and 'selfhood'. In the Threefold Alliance the human, faery, and creature allies are conscious through one another while retaining individuality in their own realms.

4 While in Yorkshire, a friend of mine was under threat of violence. I would
not be able to protect this friend against a physical attack from more than
one person, which seemed possible at the time. I thought that it would
be helpful to set an ally to watch and protect through the night, though
I was not sure if one would agree to do so. While going through the
linking process that puts the seer into direct contact with allies, I saw with
my inner vision (the Second Sight) a line of *sidh* hills, or ancient burial
mounds. To my astonishment, one of these hills broke open, and a
gigantic warrior figure on a horse emerged, shaking dirt from his shoulders. This being rode straight towards me, seeming to be both huge and
of human size at the same time. At first he seemed to be in silver armour,
but as he drew close the armour seemed to be part of him, a skin rather
than a suit. The warrior had no human feature, but a head that seemed to
shift shape, often appearing like a flower, a star, or a multiple headed axe.
This was a new type of ally for me, never seen before.

He spoke to me and said that he would stand guard, if I agreed to give in
return whatever he asked for. Though I had some doubts, I knew that if I
wanted this warrior to be an ally, I must respond without delay, and I agreed.
He said that he would tell me if anyone fitting the description that was in
my mind approached the house, and then he seemed to merge with the
building, yet also to maintain a presence in the car park below.

The next morning I experienced a strong and disturbing agitation, like
someone wrenching my stomach around. It was not a type of communication
that I had experienced before, but I knew that it meant that someone
matching my description was coming to the apartment. About ten minutes
later the bell rang, but it was a visitor for someone else in the apartment, and
quite harmless. He fitted the general height, build, and colour of the image
I had shown to the ally the night before. I experienced some amusement,
both mine and the ally's (after all, don't most humans look identical to one
another so you can't tell them apart?).

Later that day, in less tense circumstances, I attuned to the ally again. He
appeared as before, in giant form upon a powerful horse. I asked him what
my part of the bargain was to be, and he replied that it was a very great price
to pay, and must never once be forgotten. Of course I was worried, but I
had agreed. He made me swear that whenever I took people into the faery
realm, I must play music.

This ally has continued to work with me, and has been seen independently
by others at group events without previous description. One last detail seems
worth describing: across the valley from the apartment where my friend and
I stayed that night were some hills, with ancient burial mounds in them. Yet

I did not know this when I had the vision of the sidh warrior, and it was a dark winter's night.

Working with Companions

In the vast collection of folk tales (loosely called Fairy Tales today) amassed by the Grimm brothers in 19th century Denmark and Germany, there is one called *The Six Servants*. This motif is found around our world in many variants, in many cultures. It involves a man or woman acquiring supernatural allies, companions, or helpers(20). The fairy-tale of the Six Servants gives us an insight into the benefits conferred by fairy allies upon the pure of heart. We can only deal with the barest summary of the story here, but many versions are found in collections of European folk tales, including the edited and full versions from the Grimm collection itself.

A young man (a prince) falls in love with the daughter of a vicious sorceress, who murders her daughter's suitors by beheading them when they fail the Threefold tests that she sets. The prince becomes ill for seven years when his father forbids him to court the sorceress' daughter. Eventually the father gives way, and on the road to the sorceress' hall, the young man encounters six companions, who offer to be his servants. They are most unusual beings.

The first is, when he chooses, of immense size with an unlimited appetite. The second can hear all that passes in the world, even the grass growing. The third is very long, and can make himself three thousand times as long and tall as the highest mountain. The fourth has to keep a cover over his eyes, as the power of his glance shatters everything he looks upon. The fifth grows colder as the weather grows hotter...on ice he cannot breathe for the heat, in the middle of a furnace he freezes bitterly. The sixth has a long neck and keen eyes that can see to the very end of the world. Each of these companions helps the young man to gain his love, by using their special abilities to overcome the tests and tricks of the sorceress. (Please read the rest of the tale for yourself in the next pages)

These six companions or servants are of typical classes or types of fairy being widely reported. Four of them are consistent with Robert Kirk's descriptions of fairy tradition in 17th century Scotland: the great-eater (1), the shattering-sight (4), the power of opposites (cold when hot, winter when summer and so forth)(5), and of course the far-sighted (6).

In fairy magic and the Underworld tradition of Northern and Western European, as in Siberian shamanism and other chthonic traditions worldwide (but not deriving from them, as each tradition develops according to its own land and human participants), allies of this sort were frequently sought. In the folk-tale, they lend their help for a good cause, that of a young man's love against the evil magic of a sorceress; when he and his lover are married, they take their leave 'at the church door', saying that he has no further need of them. This is a typically rationalised teaching: the companions each appeared voluntarily along the road which the young man took, even though he knew that his adventure might lead to his death. They helped him through many tests and trials, and when he married his true love, departed.

The deepest levels of the tale are a spiritual drama concerning the soul and its harmony or partnership of masculine and feminine forces. It may be taken as an initiatory narrative with the road leading to possible death, the acquiring of supernatural allies, the tests set by the Dark Mother, the liberation of the Lover, and marriage of polarities. The union of male and female causes the companions to leave, for what happens next is upon a new cycle of realisation.

Here is the story of *The Six Servants* from one of the many translations and popular editions of the Grimm's collection.

The Six Servants

In olden times there lived a Queen who was a wicked sorceress and whose daughter was the loveliest girl under the sun. The old woman's only thought was how she could snare men to ruin, and when a suitor appeared, she would say no one except the man who could solve a certain problem should have her daughter. Many were dazzled by the beauty of the girl, and tried to perform the impossible task set them by the old sorceress, but always without success, and each had been obliged to kneel at her feet and have his head cut off.

A certain young Prince then heard of the girl's beauty, and said to his father, "I beg you, let me go and win her."

"Never, never," answered the King. "If you go, you go to certain death."

So the son took to his bed and was an invalid for seven years, and no doctor did him the least good.

When his father saw there was no hope of his getting better he said sorrowfully, "Go if you like and try your luck. I don't know what else to advise."

So the son got up from his couch, perfectly well, and set out in gay spirits.

It happened that as he rode over a common he saw something on the ground in front like a great mound. This, when he came nearer, proved to be a very stout fellow who was lying stretched on the ground.

The fat man, when he saw the horseman, stood up and said: "If you want anyone as a servant, take me."

The Prince asked, "What could I do with such a clumsy attendant?"

"Oh", said the fat man, "that's nothing to you so long as I behave myself well. If I like I can make myself a thousand times fatter."

"If that's the case," said the Prince, "come with me; I think you may serve my purpose."

So he went on, followed by the fat man. At a little distance he came to another man lying stretched on the grass with his ear pressed against the ground.

"What are you doing?" asked the Prince.

"I am listening," answered the man.

"And what are you listening to so attentively?"

"I am listening to all that is going on in the world. I have such keen hearing that nothing escapes me. I can even hear the grass grow."

"Well, I should like to know," said the Prince, "what you hear going on at the court of the old Queen with the beautiful daughter. Can you tell me?"

"Yes. I hear the swish of the sword that is being sharpened to cut off a suitor's head."

Then the King's son said, "You will be useful to me, so come along."

So the three pursued their road.

Next a pair of feet was seen in the distance, and parts of the legs could be seen also, but the rest was invisible. After walking a good way they came to the body and the head too.

"Good gracious!" exclaimed the Prince, "what a long Tom you are!"

"Yes," was the answer, "but when I stretch my limbs out properly I am three thousand times as long, and taller than the highest mountain on earth. If you'll engage me, I'll serve you well."

"Come along, then," replied the Prince. "You may be useful."

So they all went on together and came to a man sitting by the roadside with his eyes bound up. The Prince asked if he had weak eyes and was unable to bear the light.

"No, indeed," he answered. "I have such marvellously sharp sight that I am obliged to keep the bandage on; otherwise everything I looked at would dash to bits. If such a gift is of any service to you, take me with you."

"Come along," said the Prince. "You may be useful."

They went on and next came across a man lying in the sun, shivering and shaking as if he were frozen. Not a limb of him was still.

"What makes you shiver?" asked the Prince. "The sun is so hot."

"Ah," answered the man, "my nature is different from other people's. The warmer the weather the colder I am and the more I shiver; and when the weather is cold I become hot. On ice I cannot breathe for heat, and in the middle of a furnace I am so cold I don't know what to do."

"You are a wonderful fellow certainly," said the Prince. "If you would like to be my servant, come along."

They went on and came to a man with such a long neck that he was standing peering round him over all the mountains.

"What are you looking at so intently?" asked the Prince.

"I have such bright, keen eyes," he replied, "that I can see over woods and fields, mountains and valleys, to the very end of the world."

The Prince then said, "Come with me. It would not do to pass by such a curiosity."

Soon the Prince with his six extraordinary servants arrived in the town where the old Queen lived. Without saying who he was, he told the Queen that if she gave him her lovely daughter he would fulfil any task she might impose on him.

The sorceress was delighted at another fine and gallant youth falling into her snare, and said, "I will make a threefold condition; fulfil it, and you shall be my daughter's lord and husband."

"What is the first part?" asked the Prince.

"You are to bring me a ring that I have dropped into the bottom of the Red Sea."

The Prince went home to his servants and said, "The first thing to be done is not easy. A ring must be fished out of the Red Sea. How is it to be accomplished?"

The man with the bright eyes said, "I'll look and see the spot it lies on." He looked and announced that he saw the ring hanging on a sharp stone.

The tall, lanky man said, "I could easily fetch it out if I could see it."

"If that's all," cried the fat man, "I can help." He stooped down and held his mouth open over the water. The waves broke into it as if it had been a cave, and so he drank up the whole sea and left it as dry as a meadow.

Then the long man stooped a little and picked up the ring with his hand.

The Prince in high delight took the ring to the old sorceress.

She was naturally astounded and said, "Yes, that's the right ring. The first part of the condition you have accomplished; now comes the second. Do you see over there, grazing on the meadow in front of my castle, three hundred fat oxen? These you are to devour, hair, horns, bones and all. And in the cellars below are three hundred casks of wine. These you must drink every drop of, otherwise I shall have you killed."

"Mayn't I invite a guest to the banquet?" asked the Prince. "Without company no meal is very appetizing.

The old woman laughed evilly.

"You may invite one person," she said, "but only one."

The Prince returned to his servants and said to the fat man, "You are to be my guest to-day and eat yourself full for once."

The fat man then unbelted himself and became a thousand times bigger. He had no trouble in putting away the three hundred oxen, and when he had swallowed the last bone asked if there were not another course. He then drank all the wine out of the casks, not leaving so much as a drop hanging on the tap.

The old woman exclaimed, when she learnt that he had performed the second part of the condition, "So far no one else has done as much as you! But now comes the third point, and this is the hardest of all and will certainly cost you your head."

Then she said, "This evening I shall bring my daughter to your room and leave her there, and you may sit with your arms round her. But be careful that you keep awake. I shall come again at twelve, and if in the meantime she has vanished you are lost."

The Prince thought, "This part of the condition sounds easy and pleasant. I shall not be likely to close my eyes." He nevertheless called his servants and confided in them what the old creature had said.

"There is no knowing what cunning lies behind the proposal," he remarked. "One cannot be too careful. So keep watch and be careful that the maiden doesn't escape from my chamber."

At nightfall the sorceress brought her daughter and put her in the Prince's arms; then the lanky one twisted himself in a circle round the pair, and the fat man stationed himself at the door so that no living soul could come in. There the two sat and the girl did not speak a word, but the moonlight shone through the window and lit up her lovely face. The Prince could do nothing but look at her beauty, full of joy and love, and no fatigue visited his eyes. This lasted till eleven o'clock, when the old queen cast a spell over them and they all fell asleep, and at that moment the girl was taken away. They slept on till a quarter to twelve, when the spell lost its power and they awoke.

"Oh, misery and misfortune," cried the Prince. "Now I am lost indeed."

The faithful servants began to wring their hands, but the listener with the sharp hearing said, "All be quiet and let me listen."

He listened for a moment, and then reported: "She is sitting within a rock three hundred hours' journey from here and laments her fate. You alone can help her, lanky one; two or three strides will take you there."

"Yes," answered the lanky one, "but the sharp-eyed man must come also to smash down the rocks."

So the lanky man picked up the man with the bandage over his eyes, and in a second, before you had time to snap your fingers, they were standing by the enchanted rock. At once the lanky man removed the bandage from his companion's sharp eyes, and with one glance the rock was shivered to atoms. The lanky man then took the maiden up, carried her back in a moment, went again for his comrade, and just as twelve struck they were all in their places as they had been before the spell..

The old sorceress slunk in with a sneering smile, as much as to say, "Now he must be mine," for she thought her daughter hundreds of miles away inside the rock. But when she saw the girl in the Prince's arms she was frightened and muttered, "Here's a man who can do greater wonders than I."

There was nothing now to be done but to give her daughter to the Prince. But she managed to whisper in her ear, "Shame on you to obey the behests of vulgar people; not to choose your bridegroom of your own free will."

The maiden's proud soul now rose in revolt and she planned revenge. Next morning she ordered three hundred faggots of wood to be collected and set alight, and said that although the threefold condition had been fulfilled she would not marry the Prince till one of his party had sat in the midst of the burning faggots. She imagined not one of the servants would consent to burn for their master's sake, and that he out of love for her would get into the fire himself, and so she would be rid of him.

The servants said to one another, "We have all done something except the shivering fellow; now it is his turn."

So they sent him into the furnace. It burnt for three days, and when the flames subsided there stood the shivering man among the ashes, shaking like an aspen-leaf, blue with cold.

"Such a frost," he said, "I have never experienced in all my life. If it had gone on much longer I should have been frozen to death."

Now there was no escape; the beautiful girl was obliged to take the strange youth for her husband. But when he was leading her to the church the old Queen said, "I cannot bear this disgrace," and she called out the soldiers and sent them to the church to bring back her daughter.

The listener, however, had pricked up his ears and heard what the old woman was saying privately to her officers.

"What shall we do?" he said to the fat man.

The latter was ready with a plan, which was to pour out of his mouth a part of the Red Sea that he had swallowed, and this was enough to drown all the armed knights that came riding up to the church.

When the sorceress knew this she sent out large reinforcements, but these fared no better, for the sharp-eyed man took off his bandage and looked at them, and they fell to bits like broken glass.

Now the ceremony proceeded without interruption, and when it was over the six servants took their leave at the church door.

"Your desires are now all fulfilled," they said to their master. "You have no further need of us; we will therefore travel on and seek our fortune,"

Half an hour's walk from the Prince's castle there was a village where a swineherd was tending his pigs.

"Do you know what I really am?" the bridegroom asked his wife. "I am not a Prince at all, but a swineherd like that man over there, who is my father. You and I must go and help him now to feed the pigs."

So he alighted with her at the inn and gave instructions that in the night her royal garments were to be taken away, and the landlady gave her a pair of coarse woollen stockings and an old petticoat to put on.

In the morning when she woke up the Princess thought, "I have deserved all this because I have been so proud and haughty," and she quite believed her husband was a swineherd and she went out with him to feed the pigs.

This lasted eight days, and by the end of that time her feet were torn and sore, and she wondered how she could stand it longer. Then some people came one day and asked if she knew who her husband really was, and she said, "Yes, he is a swineherd, and is just gone to drive a bargain in the town."

They then said, "Come with us and we will take you to him." They led her up to the castle, and in the entrance hall her husband stood waiting to welcome her, attired in royal clothes.

At first she did not recognize him, but he took her in his arms and kissed her and said, "I suffered for you so much and now you have suffered a little for me."

Then the wedding feast was given in good earnest, and I wish you and I had been there.

Faeries,
Extraterrestrials,
Angels

'In times before Christ there were Druids here who enchanted one another with Druid rods made of brass, and metamorphosed one another into stone and lumps of oak. The question is, Where are the spirits of these Druids now? Their spirits are wafted through the air, and the man or beast they meet is smitten, while their own bodies are still under enchantment. I had such a Druid enchantment in my hand; it wasn't stone, nor marble, nor flint, and had human shape. It was found in the centre of a big rock on Innis-na-Gore; and round this rock light used to appear at night. The man who owned the stone decided to blast it up, and he found at its centre the enchantment – just like a man, with head and legs and arms. Father Healy took the enchantment away, when he was here on a visit, and said that it was a Druid enchanted, and that to get out of the rock was one part of the releasement, and that there would be a second and complete releasement of the Druid.'

The Fairy Tribes Classified.— Finally I asked Patrick to classify, as far as he could, all the fairy tribes he had ever heard about, and he said:- 'The leprechaun is a red-capped fellow who stays round pure springs, generally shoemaking for the rest of the fairy tribes. The lunantishees are the tribes that guard the blackthorn trees or sloes; they let you cut no stick on the eleventh of November (the original November Day), or on the eleventh of May (the original May Day). If at such a time you cut a blackthorn, some misfortune will come to you. Pookas are black-featured fellows mounted on good horses; and are horse-dealers. They visit racecourses, but usually are invisible. The gentry are the most noble tribe of all; and they are a big race who came from the planets – according to my idea; they usually appear white. The Daoine Maithe (though there is some doubt, the same or almost the same as the gentry) were next to Heaven at the Fall, but did not fall; they are a people expecting salvation.'

From *The Fairy Faith in Celtic Countries*,
W Y Evans Wentz, 1911.

Young Tame Lin, or Tamlane

The subject of the ballad Young Tam Lin, of which there are many versions, both in the Border country and in Aberdeenshire, is perhaps the most important of all the supernatural ballads because of the many fairy beliefs incorporated in it. The fullest version is No.39A in Child's *The English and Scottish Popular Ballads*. At the beginning the king warns the maidens in his court not to go to Carterhaugh Wood, which is haunted by Young Tam Lin who exacts a pledge from every maiden who visits it, most likely her maidenhood. In spite of his warning, his own daughter Janet goes to the well of Carterhaugh, summons Young Tam Lin by plucking a rose, and loses her maidenhood to him. The rest of the ballad is so vivid and so full of important detail that it would be a pity only to summarize it.

> Janet has kilted her green kirtle
>   A little aboon her knee,
>   And she has snooded her yellow hair,
>   A little aboon her bree,
>   And she is to her father's ha,
>   As fast as she can hie.
>
> Four and twenty ladies fair
>   Were playing at the ba,
>   And out then cam the fair Janet,
>   Ance the flower amang them a'.
>
> Four and twenty ladies fair
>   Were playing at the chess,
>   And out then cam the fair Janet,
>   As green as onie glass.
>   Out then spak an ault grey knight,
>   Lay oer the castle wa,
>   And says, Alas, fair Janet, for thee
>   But we'll be blamed a'.
>
> 'Haud your tongue, ye auld fac'd knight,
>   Some ill death may ye die!
>   Father my bairn on whom I will,
>   I'll father nane on thee.'
>
> Out then spak her father dear,
>   And he spak meek and mild;
>   'And ever alas, sweet Janet,' he says,
>   'I think thou gaes wi child.'

'If that I gae wi child, father,
　　Mysel maun bear the blame;
　　There's neer a laird about your ha
　　Shall get the bairn's name.

'If my love were an earthly knight,
　　As he's an elfin grey,
　　I wad na gie my ain true-love
　　For nae lord that ye hae.

'The steed that my true-love rides on
　　Is lighter than the wind;
　　Wi siller he is shod before,
　　Wi burning gowd behind.'

Janet has kilted her green kirtle
　　A little aboon her knee,
　　And she has snooded her yellow hair
　　A little aboon her bree,
　　And she's awa to Carterhaugh
　　As fast as she can hie.

When she cam to Carterhaugh,
　　Tam Lin was at the well,
　　And there she fand his steed standing,
　　But away was himsel.

She had na pu'd a double rose,
　　A rose but only twa,
　　Till up then started young Tam Lin,
　　Says Lady, thou pu's nae mae.

Why pu's thou the rose, Janet,
　　Amang the groves sae green,
　　And a' to kill the bonnie babe
　　That we gat us between?

'O tell me, tell me, Tam Lin,' she says,
　　'For's sake that died on tree,
　　If eer ye was in holy chapel,
　　Or christendom did see?'

'Roxbrugh he was my grandfather,
  Took me with him to bide,
  And ance it fell upon a day
  That wae did me betide.

'And ance it fell upon a day,
  A cauld day and a snell,
  When we were frae the hunting come
  That frae my horse I fell;
  The Queen o Fairies she caught me,
  In yon green hill to dwell.

'But the night is Halloween, lady,
  The morn is Hallowday;
  Then win me, win me, an ye will,
  For weel I wat ye may.

'Just at the mirk and midnight hour
  The fairy folk will ride,
  And they that wad their true-love win,
  At Miles Cross they maun bide.'

'But how shall I thee ken, Tam Lin,
  Or how my true-love know,
  Amang sae mony unco knights
  The like I never saw?'

'O first let pass the black, lady,
  And syne let pass the brown,
  But quickly run to the milk-white steed,
  Pu ye his rider down.

'For I'll ride on the milk-white steed,
  And ay nearest the town;
  Because I was an earthly knight
  They gie me that renown.

'My right hand will be glovd, lady,
  My left hand will be bare,
  Cockt up shall my bonnet be,
  And kaimd down shall my hair,
  And thae's the takens I gie thee,
  Nae doubt I will be there.

'They'll turn me in your arms, lady,
   Into an esk and adder;
   But hold me fast, and fear me not,
   I am your bairn's father.

'They'll turn me to a bear sae grim,
   And then a lion bold;
   But hold me fast, and fear me not,
   As ye shall love your child.

'Again they'll turn me in your arms
   To a red het gaud of airn;
   But hold me fast, and fear me not,
   I'll do to you nae harm.

'And last they'll turn me in your arms
   Into the burning gleed;
   Then throw me into well water,
   O throw me in wi speed.

'And then I'll be your ain true-love,
   I'll turn a naked knight;
   Then cover me wi your green mantle,
   And cover me out o sight.'

Gloomy, gloomy was the night,
   And eerie was the way,
   As fair Jenny in her green mantle
   To Miles Cross she did gae.

About the middle o the night
   She heard the bridles ring;
   This lady was as glad at that
   As any earthly thing.

First she let the black pass by,
   And syne she let the brown;
   But quickly she ran to the milk-white steed,
   And pu'd the rider down.

Sae weel she minded shae he did say,
   And young Tam Lin did win;
   Syne covered him wi her green mantle,
   As blythe's a bird in spring.

Out then spak the Queen o Fairies,
  Out of a bush o broom;
  'Them that has gotten young Tam Lin
  Has gotten a stately groom.'

Out then spak the Queen o Fairies,
  And an angry woman was she;
  'Shame betide her ill-far'd face,
  And an ill death may she die,
  For she's taen awa the bonniest knight
  In a' my companie.

'But had I kend, Tam Lin,' she says,
  'What now this night I see,
  I wad hae taen out thy twa grey een,
  And put in twa een o tree.'

Here we have the summoning of a spirit by breaking the branch of a tree sacred to him, the FAIRY RADE with its jingling bells at Hallowe'en, the time most sacred to the fairies, the fairy KNOWE, the TEIND to Hell – so characterisitic of Scottish Fairyland – the rescue from Fairyland by holding fast, the SHAPE-SHIFTING of the captive, and the essential ill-will of the Fairy Queen.

Tamlin, Tamlane, Tam-a-Lin were names often given to a fairy, sometimes a page, sometimes a knight and sometimes a grotesquely comic character, as in the nursery rhyme:

Tam-a-Lin and his wife, and his wife's mother,
  They went over a bridge all three together;
  The bridge was broken, and they fell in;
  'The devil go with all!' says Tam-a-Lin.

From K Briggs, A Dictionary of Fairies with
Ballad Text from F.J. Child,
The English and Scottish Popular Ballads.

Scottish seers in Virginia

It has been reported by Kirk, Tarbett, and others, that the seer or seeress loses the Second Sight upon arrival in the Colonies. I have discussed this with the learned Johnson who affirmed it to be nonsense, though he had evidence of the Sight while on his much vaunted Tour of the Highlands and Islands. Yet learned clergy and men of science have described this loss, and conversely the gaining of the Sight through remaining in one place for many years, as if the man and the land become part of one another, causing clarification of the eye.

In 1744 I determined to pursue this topic myself upon my arrival in Virginia, where there had long been an underclass of Gaels, recently restocked by land enclosures and deportations from the Highlands. It was easy to find these wretches for most of them were in enclosed areas and had their movement restricted by the Crown governors. Many of these were bondservants, slaves in effect, and treated like blacks. Others were used as a source of irregular labour day by day. The pitiable conditions in which they lived were even more wretched than the turf hovels in which they had eked out their miserable lives in Scotland or Ireland, so they longed for the poverty and degradation of their homelands from which the English landlords had sent them.

I saw aged men with long white hair down to the waist and beard to the chest all uncombed, some with little packets tied into them for safety, perhaps tobacco or herbs or a coin. There were women and children in meagre rags, scarcely decent, their thin bodies burned red under the sun from long hours of field work. They lived in huts of stick and mud, crammed into single rooms, in filth, vermin, and starvation. When they died the local military charged a fee for paupers unnamed burial without service, for they were all Catholic or Episcopalian. There were some in utter slavery to work off the charges to bury their loved ones.

As I walked through the camp, none would speak with me. Indeed, they seemed to melt into the mire, vanishing silently as I approached. This was in contrast to the aggressive staring and following of the English peasants, to counter which I had wont to bear a cudgel in the more remote areas of Devon and Cornwall. These Scottish-Irish were, as I thought, a cowed and heart-crushed people.

So I accosted a youth, catching him by the hair which was the only part not covered in filth, and demanded in English that he lead me to one with the Two Sights. He stood his ground with dignity and when I let him go shook his head as if to say he had no knowledge of the language or of what I sought, yet I could tell by his eyes that he had. I gave him some tobacco to chew, which he devoured greedily stuffing it into his mouth until his cheeks were plump as a squirrel. Without speaking, either *through choice or for fear of displaying his treasure to others he led me to a stinking hut in the middle of a deep pool of dung and fetid green water. He left me standing by the skin, for there was no door to open or close, only posts with a rotten hide hanging from them.*

As I was about to call out to whoever was within, I felt something brush my face, like the touch of a spider web blown in the breeze. It seemed as if a haze or wisp of smoke passed across my line of sight, then an aged man staggered out of the hut and leaned on the doorpost nodding and trembling. Despite his weakness of limb, he looked upon me with the unblinking stare of the trained seer, and held out his black claw of a hand. I instantly gave him tobacco and a small pouch of strong tea which was a rare and valued gift. He spoke to me in English of a sort, with many words that I did not understand, and took me into the hut which was furnished only with some bags hanging from the low roof and a pile of wet straw on the floor. The elder offered me some rough bread and green milk, a great gift from one so poor, so I had to accept honourably though it tasted foul and made me fear for poisoning for days after.

After some politeness and circumlocutions, for the Gaels will never talk straight, I asked him if he Saw, and if his Sight had changed when he came into the Colonies. This is what he said:

"On arrival in this wild place, touched by the shadow of wicked men with cruelty in their hearts unwarmed by the love of God, I became blind. I saw nothing, my Sight was dead. It was like dying to be one-sighted, and no one respected me. There are true people, the children of this wild land, and they live in the great forests to the West of here and to the North. These people must be lost tribes of the Gael, for they share all things in common and love the land, and they have comimeadh or Walkers from the sith who converse with them. But these cousins would not speak with me, for I was a stranger in their land, and I think now that just as I could not see them, they could not see me, for my substance was of Uist, my home island, and not of the great wilderness here. None of my own darlings crossed the dark waters with me in the prison ship, and I was alone.

For many days and nights I was alone, and though I prayed to the sainted goddess Brigit to intercede for me with her foster son and grant me allies, none came. A local trader family took me as a house servant, and they fed me well, and I waited upon them. They had heard of my reputation, for I was a great and famous man in the Isles both for the seeing of Two Sights and the taking out of motes and eye specks and clots deep in the lung by the blessed bowl of water and holy prayers. Alas for me and my reputation, for when they found that I could make no show for them, they threw me into the pen, and found a younger man to serve them.

If my days had been dark before they were darker then than black coal wet from the sea, and for seven years I abandoned hope, and barely remembered to pray and make protections against evil thoughts. In the seventh year, I was ill with fever, which kills many here in the hot damp season. Only the charity of my clan kept me hovering upon the edge of life, and whatever was given to me was denied the mouth of another. It was then that my Sight returned, for all of Scotland was finally purged from me, and my body was wholly of the stuff of this land, weak and useless as that body was.

One night, at dawn when the wolf runs close to the camp just before the Sun rises, I came out of my fever, awakened by the sound of scratching at the doorpost. I called out, and in came a child, all covered in feathers like a little bright bird, on her arms and legs, and over her face, and spreading out in a nodding plume where a child of man would have hair. She was my first companion in this land, and she was inexperienced, not like those powers that had walked with me in strength and joy and terror in the mountains and at the sea shore at home.

That was in the summer of last year, and since then my Sight has opened out and grown stronger. I have gifts given to me again, and I can See for others, though the power to take out thorns and bullets and lung clots has not returned. The English flesh eaters have come to see me, just as you have, and asked me for visions, though the Sight does not come at command.

You are hot upon the heels of a great lord of the English army, who wanted to know what was happening in Scotland, for he had heard rumours that made him fear for his authority and power. Indeed I saw to Scotland, for my bird maiden can cross the raging ocean in an instant and lend me her eyes, though she is a mere child and cannot understand what she sees there.

I saw a fine prince on a white horse, radiant is this prince like the sun, and he rides with a vast army into England. The light of true kingship is upon him, but he has a dark shadow to advise him, one who will betray him and abandon him at the crossroads. This prince will be known forever as the Beautiful Prince, but alas and sorrow for him, and woe for him in seeking his rightful throne stolen by foreigners and farmers. I see long hardship travelling over hard rocks and cold nights in the wilderness. I see many years before he comes at last to his rightful place, three hundred or more of years before he takes his throne at the end of time, when the planets roll out of their proper Signs and the ancestors rise up to dance for him at his crowning..."

Here I stopped the old wretch in mid-flight, for he was sweating and his eyes had rolled up into their sockets. I was afraid that if he died in a fit then I would not get out of the camp without some sly hurt to myself from his countrymen. When his breathing slowed, I told him that men did not live to be three hundred years. With some difficulty of words he made clear to me that he inferred the lineage or bloodline or spirit of this mysterious prince, which was, he said, of more significance than the actual person.

Of a sudden I grasped the meaning of his vision, at least in part, for I knew that the French had been rumoured to support Charles, the Young Pretender to the English Throne, and that wild stories of a planned invasion through Scotland had been circulating the week in which I set sail for Virginia. I resolved to speak with the commanding officer of the local garrison, who would receive news by the fastest ships of any such invasion. Little wonder, I thought, as I waded through the mud to the gate of the camp, that an English officer had sought the services of the seer. If the Pretender reached into England it would be civil war, and if he got the throne we would all be ruined.

Extract from an early 18th century journal

Are Faeries Space-people?

The question about a possible connection between faeries and extraterrestrials is often asked, in letters, at talks or discussions, in workshops, and in interviews. Sometimes such questions are laden with escapism, wishful thinking, propaganda, but it is possible to attempt a serious response. Exploring the different aspects of the question and comparing older and contemporary beliefs reveals some curious and remarkable ideas. To begin unfolding the many-layered answers to the question, I should begin by briefly stating my own understanding of the situation, which is as follows: faeries are an independent life form, closely linked to the land and to the planet as a whole. This implies that they are not space-people, but it does not imply that there are no extraterrestrial beings. The rest of this chapter includes ideas and traditions that are more complex than my own brief statement, some rooted in the depths of ancestral memory and tradition, and others surfacing as modern fantasies.

I feel that many of the modern encounters with what my grandparents would have called faeries, particularly in the USA, are nowadays interpreted as meetings with, or sightings of, extraterrestrials. But this is only because there is no older tradition to tap into. Many such encounters that have been described to me are in a classic faery genre, different in many ways from the hi-tech encounters that have abounded since the spread of science-fiction in the 1950's. If the humans involved in these encounters had grown up with the older traditions rather than television, they might well have recognised the traditional nature of their adventures. I do not think (as some enthusiasts do) that all such encounters, past and present, are rationalisations of meetings with space beings, as it is abundantly clear from tradition that faery beings live within the body of the land, and do not come in vehicles from the sky.

Our modern enthusiasm for extraterrestrials began to take form around the same time that both television and science fiction became popular, and it is undoubtedly linked to the materialistic hi-tech aspirations and propaganda of the space-race in the old style political blocs of the USA and USSR. The immense following for Star Trek, originally a low budget television series, shows science fiction and fantasy filling the human need for the unknown, the otherworld, the escape. The vocabulary and imagery, however, is neither orthodox religious or traditional faery lore, but that of the era: hi-tech materialist mysticism.

There may be partial truth in an extraterrestrial theory of religious origins when we consider the widespread mythic themes of deities and superhuman beings coming from the sky. Such ideas are found in ancient traditions and religions, but to suggest, as do many enthusiasts (who have done little research) that this is the sole source of religion and mythology is reductionist nonsense. Mythology is often rationalised, psychologised, reduced, politicised, yet its profundity and power is never used up, belittled, or explained by such retrospective or simplistic interpretations. Many of the stellar themes in myth and religion are founded on long term observation of star patterns, on what we would today call synchronicity and relativity. This ancient art, the forerunner of our rather limited modern astrology, is more subtle and profound than the crude notion that all gods and goddesses were originally visitors in space vehicles.

There is also an esoteric tradition, once taught verbally and in secret, though now much popularised and trivialised, that certain branches of humanity came from the stars, and more specifically from Lyra or the Pleiades. This teaching was handed down in the old magical or Hermetic teaching orders in the Northern hemisphere as part of the Atlantean tradition, first described by Plato (though he does not mention any stellar origins for the Atlanteans).

The Egyptian civilisation, according to this tradition in its various forms, is also said to derive from an Atlantean/stellar source. Since the translation of hieroglyphics, many writers from the 19th century onwards have pointed out the importance of stellar themes in Egyptian religion, and that the 1st Dynasty pyramids are aligned towards Orion, Sirius, and relative patterns depending upon the constellation of the Bear and the Pole star.

Similarly the extensive megalithic alignments in Northern Europe, predating the oldest Egyptian pyramids, have been shown by Professor Alexander Thom(17) and others to be aligned with great accuracy to observed star patterns.

At its best this tradition, nowadays reinforced by the widely debated archaeological stellar evidence, hints that humanity is not limited to this one planet, and so it presents a deeper theory of origins than that of materialist evolution. At its worst it leads into the potential racism of the Theosophical Society and the genocide of the Nazi theory and practice concerning inferior and superior races.

In other words the supposedly superior white Aryan races were the descendants of the star people, while the inferior others were the sub-humanity whom they visited and dragged up from savagery to be their slaves. This would be amusing if it were not so dangerous. The same idea is found in other forms, and we can put it into perspective through religious and political variants of the 'master-race' theme. In Britain and Europe the old style historians and archaeologists taught that the superior Romans came in and civilised the ignorant savage Celts; in the USA the native tribes were supposed to be inferior; while in India the English Dutch and Portuguese used similar excuses for their destruction and imperialism. In Scotland and

Ireland, where the English banned all traditional culture, the Gaels or Celts were regarded as inferior sub-humans, while in England as late as the 19th century there were publications and discussions on the question: 'are the lower classes human ?'. The list could be extended wherever we find humanity excusing its prejudices and greed.

So when we find New Age channellers talking about the ascended Masters and the Pleiadians who steer the history of humanity, we are not simply encountering wishful thinking or commercialised fantasy for the masses. Firstly there is an ancient tradition, found worldwide, that humanity came from the stars. Secondly it has been abused as an excuse for racial superiority, just as religion and politics and tribalism are used in a similar way.

What is particularly significant is that the tradition of the Pleiades is still active today in the folklore and wisdom teachings of some isolated races in the Southern hemisphere, among primal peoples who have never seen an occult book or (praise be!) heard a New Age channelling tape. Such people tell that they came from the Pleiades long ago in ships.

The rising and setting of the small star group of Pleiades is used worldwide to mark the pivot of the year, for when they rise in the Northern hemisphere they are setting in the Southern, and vice versa. The modern dates for this relativistic event are close to May 1st and November 5th, the Celtic feasts of Beltane and Samhain, or May day and Halloween, the two portal fire-festivals. These so-called Celtic, but truly pre-Celtic, festival dates are not, as is often stated incorrectly, solar events. The Celts did not use a solar calender, but a lunar one. Nor did the pre-Celtic and megalithic people base their time patterns on the seasons and the sun, but upon stellar and planetary patterns linked together.

The portals or thresholds of May and November (sometimes called cross-quarters when linked to the solar year) were found originally through observation of the Pleiades as they appeared or disappeared over the horizon, just as they are observed today by primal peoples who still follow the old stellar patterns. This ancient and enduring tradition may be one of the strongest suggestions of evidence linking humanity and the stars: yet Beltane and Samhain, the Pleiades festivals, are also potent times for faery and ancestral contact, when the faery hosts ride over the surface of the land, and meet humans face to face. So we come to the link between faeries and ancestors, with the added traditional teaching that some of the ancestors came from other worlds, from distant planets in a specific star group.

What seems to occur in May and November, marked by the setting and rising of the Pleiades is a subtle planetary energy shift. This is dependent upon many relative factors, synchronous with, and possibly including, the visibility of the Pleiades. In other words our planet reaches a relative position in the solar system, and the system itself reaches a relative position, which for us is marked by the sight of the Pleiades ascending or descending over the horizon. What these energetic factors are in modern physics-speak we do not claim to know, but in tradition these thresholds of the year occasion great tides of energy and an opening of the gates between the realms or dimensions.

The Riding, or Faery Host, or Wild Hunt gathering souls, occurs in November, at a time nowadays called Samhain after a Celtic feast name for the season, or Halloween in the popular tradition. It is a feast of the Ancestors, the Underworld, and the wild aspect of the faery hosts. In the ballad *Tam Lin* it is the time when mortals are rescued from the faery realm, when the Host or Court rides across the surface of the land. Robert Kirk describes something similar of the Quarter days in the Highlands, when the Gaels would come to church to avoid the Host travelling the highways. As a feast of the dead, the time of November 11th (approximately) was celebrated in the ancient world with rituals, prohibitions, and many traditional and religious teachings.

In May, nowadays May 1st, Beltane or May Day, but actually sometime around May 5th-11th, the goddess Brigit brought in the fire of rebirth, of fertility, courtship, and the opening of Summer. In the Highlands and Ireland, this feast of Brigit was associated with sacred mounds, serpents, sexuality, and the powers of protection and Light. So the November tide is one of death, and the May tide is one of rebirth. As these thresholds are celebrated worldwide with similar traditions (though with different deities and cultural and environmental attributes) they are more than mere superstition.

Faeries and Angels

In workshops, talks, and in letters from around the world, people often ask about the relationship between angels and faeries. My answer is that they do indeed have a relationship, but that we must first understand their differences before we can understand where they connect with and relate to each other. The illustration, figure 1, shows the idea of overworld and underworld beings handed down in tradition, with humanity upon the surface of the planet partaking of both above and below. Much of our individual, collective, and environmental and planetary imbalance is through rejection of the underworld, rather than of the overworld.

The propagandist Christianized idea of escape from 'material bondage' is pernicious and deeply damaging to humanity. The direct result of this idea is, paradoxically, materialism; all is dead, usable, exploitable, discardable.

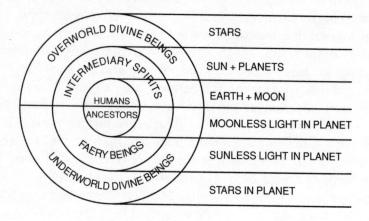

Figure 1 Overworld and Underworld inhabitants

And so we destroy our planet, because we have been convinced that the Earth is not a living being, that we are not part of her, she is not within us.

This rejection of the manifest world is at the very core of our ills and imbalances, be they individual or planetary. Our current lack of understanding of the true nature of both faery beings and angels illustrates this rejection, particularly through our self- protective trivialisation.

At one time, not so long ago, the differences between faeries and angels were amply described in various traditions, with varying degrees of Judaeo-Christian emphasis and propaganda. Today there is much confusion, and the boundaries between faeries and angels, well described in both folklore and esoteric traditions, are blurred in the general imagination. This blurring is, ironically, due to our lack of knowledge of the nature of angels, and the collapse of Christianity, rather than to our revival of interest in faeries.

In the Gnostic gospels (18), two orders of angels are described: the angels of the Father Above, in the Heavens, and the angels of the Mother Below, in the Earth. These angels of the goddess in the Earth might be faeries, and we shall return to this idea later. The angels of the Father, however, are most definitely not faeries, and we should briefly establish what they are before making our comparison, and before examining the modern confusion between angels and faeries.

The Judaic and Christian traditions, and their close relative the Islamic tradition, all describe angels in detail. The most detailed sources are probably Kabbalistic, for in Kabbalah the esoteric mystical and magical arts of the

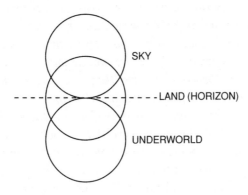

Figure 1b   The three worlds or Environments

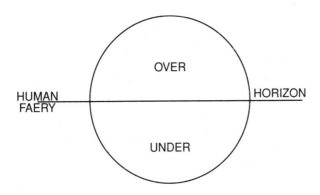

Figure 1c   The mirroring of human and faery realms

Semitic traditions are found. Kabbalah also permeates Northern Europe, via Greek, Celtic and Norse traditions, particularly the Neo-Platonic and Hermetic traditions that inherited the wisdom of pagan Europe and preserved it through the centuries of Christianity. Thus we have both orthodox and unorthodox descriptions of angels to draw upon. We can hardly do better for an example than begin with the vision of Ezekiel, from the Old Testament:-

And I looked and behold, four wheels beside the cherubim, one wheel beside one cherub, and another wheel beside another cherub, and the appearance of the wheels was as the colour of a beryl stone. And as for their appearance, they four had one likeness, as if a wheel had been within a wheel. When they went they went upon their four sides, they turned not as they went, but to the place whither the head looked they followed it; they turned not as they went. And their whole body, and their backs, and their hands, and their wings, and the wheels, were full of eyes round about, even the wheels that they four had. As for the wheels they were called in my hearing, the whirling wheels. And every one had four faces, the first face was the face of the cherub, and the second face was the face of a man, and the third the face of a lion, and the fourth the face of an eagle. And the cherubim mounted up: this is the living creature that I saw by the river Chebar. (Ezekiel 10, 9–15).

The cherubim (plural of cherub or kerub) are not the pretty little baby creatures of sentiment, but beings of great power and multiple form. The angelic Kerubim are, in one sense, living forms of the power of the four Elements of Air, Fire, Water, and Earth. Ezekiel's vision of the Kerubim is in the Kabbalistic tradition of the powers of the Kingdom, the realm of Divinity inherent within the planet Earth, the Sacred Land. Yet these are clearly not, if we compare traditions, faery beings, who are also inherent within the land. They are the angels of the Father in Heaven come to Earth, and during the vision they are described as having both the power of flight (wings) and the power of manipulation, a hand beneath each wing. The kerubim mirror the stellar or originative Holy Living Creatures that are uttered in and out of the Void, sometimes called the Four Aeons, the Four Powers of Life, Light, Love, and Law, which are before the Throne of Being.

In Kabbalistic mysticism (19) the appearances of other angels are similarly shocking and paradoxical: Seraphim as fiery serpents with many eyes and flaming swords, Ophanim as wheels rimmed with eyes, Aishim as shimmering lights between birth and death, Malakim as flaming lines of light, uttered by the Sun, and so forth. In fact angels, in all the Middle Eastern traditions such as Christianity, are messengers or carriers or annunciators of the Word, the power of Divinity. Furthermore, they are intimately part of the solar system, and linked to the traditional planets of Venus, Mercury, Mars, Jupiter, Saturn, the Sun, and the Moon. They are beings that embody the consciousness of the Solar Logos, the living Being which is physically present as the Sun, and which has its planetary bodies that define its powers, phases, and spheres of energy.

So there are angels of the planet Earth (Kerubim), the Moon (Aishiim), Mercury (Bene-elohim), Venus (Elohim), the Sun (Malakim), Mars (Seraphim), Jupiter (Chasmalim), Saturn (Aralim), Neptune or the Zodiac, (Ophanim), and the primal Being (Chioth ha Kaddesh, the Holy Living Creatures). Each order of angels is associated with a planetary Archangel, and here we find a significant connection to some of the traditions of faery races, for the totality of the angels of any sphere (see figure 2, the Tree of Life) is the Archangel of that Sphere. In other words angels and archangels are collective beings, just as some faeries arc hive beings. In Kabbalah all the

Archangels together make up the parts of a body, and so have correspondences to the human organism, which is a miniature of the solar system, the organism of the Solar Logos.

Just as we have the idea of collective beings as angels and archangels associated with the planets, and the whole being the body of the Solar Being, so do we have the idea of these as wheels as described by Ezekiel. The entire solar entity is the Sun, the planets that orbit around it, and the lesser bodies of moons, asteroids, fragments and so forth. These are, in total, the body of the Solar Being. It is made up of ceaseless motion, many parts orbiting that make up the whole. Our Earth and Moon are part of that body, influenced by all the other parts, and the whole solar being relates to other stars as it travels through the universe.

The wheels are the perimeters of the Spheres of Being. These are the limits of the planetary orbits in one sense, while in a universal or metaphysical sense they are the Three Rings of Time, Space, and Events. These three rings or wheels are the fundamentals of relativity, though the idea was taught in the Mysteries, in Kabbalah, and in the Hermetic traditions, long before Einstein gave it a modern vocabulary. Thus when we find angels and archangels described as Wheels (Ophanim), Spokes or Rays (Malakim), Hollows, thrones or vessels (Aralim) and so forth, they are the defining limits and powers of the solar being.

In religious and mystical traditions, encounters with angels are difficult, they are often terrifying in power and appearance, and always have both a cosmological and a metaphysical nature. Angelic descriptions are traditionally in a vocabulary of planetary mysticism, such as the Kabbalah, leading from Earth to Stars, via Sun, Moon and Planets. This is highly developed in the Gnostic hymns and invocations.

More recently angels have been recast in a false New Age mould. They have become sugary, ethereal, white robed beings who pull us out of difficulties or encourage us with religious platitudes. Angels are said to guard our houses, to protect us on the way to the supermarket, to heal our cancerous pets, to be ready to pull the elect out of the nuclear holocaust, to etherealise a grubby and gross humanity. None of this bears any relationship to what angels are described as doing, as being, in the Judaic and Islamic traditions, including Christianity and its variants. Since the Christian orthodox churches started to down-play the role of angels, their true nature has been forgotten. Who reads those complex visions in the Bible now?

So the popular fate of angels is the same as that of faeries, for they have been trivialised. Angels are overworld powers, beings that embody the Mind and Energies of the Solar Being, which is itself a Star. Faeries are underworld powers, beings that embody the Mind and Energies of stellar life inherent

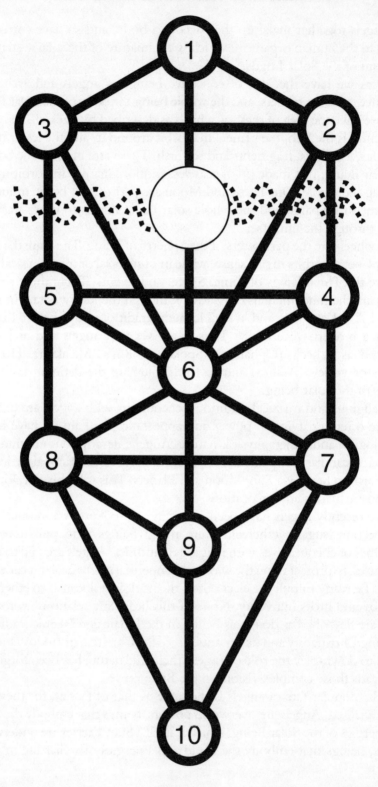

Figure 2   The Tree of Life.

1) Original Source of Being out of Non-Being. The first breath of the universe, the seed of consciousness and energy. This Sphere is Neutral, balanced, or pre-polarisation. The CROWN of the Tree of Life.

2) WISDOM: primal power in motion. Associated with active analalytic 'male' divine energy. The utterance of the World or Worlds.

3) UNDERSTANDING: primal vessel that contains power. Associated with catalytic receptive 'female' divine energy. The Great Mother.

4) MERCY (The Giver): a reflection or harmonic of (2) in which the energies of creation issue across the Abyss. The positive anabolic male power of giving-out. This power works upon a cosmic level; it is the building force of creation.

5) SEVERITY (The Taker): harmonic vessel of (3). Catabolic, receptive, female. Represented in traditions worldwide by a severe female divinity often of fierce aspect. The cosmic destroying force, breaking down and purifying. Frequently ascribed to a male god-form (Mars) in relatively modern literature, due to misunderstanding of the polarity of the Tree pattern.

6) CENTRALITY or BEAUTY or HARMONY: balanced fusion of all energies. Ahermaphrodite or bi-sexual power which reflects the Crown and acts as the central focus for all energies below the Abyss which separates the upper Triad (1/2/3) from the remainder of the Tree. Traditionally this is the realm of the saviour, the Sons of Light, the Divine Kings. It also represents the Sun of our solar system.

7) VICTORY: the Young Goddess or Flower Maiden. The emotions. An anabolic active aphere. Associated with Venus traditionally.

8) HONOUR: the young god. The intellect. A catabolic receptive male power. Both Honour and Victory exchange polarities. Associated with Hermes.

9) FOUNDATION: male and female united. The matrix of expressed life forms and materialised energy; all previous Spheres fuse together. Associated with the Moon goddesses and gods.

10)KINGDOM: the expressed world drawn from all of the foregoing. Paradoxically this world is closest to the CROWN.

THREE PILLARS DEFINED

There are Three Pillars or polarisations overall; left, right, centre. The Central Pillar (which is the spindle of the sphere of the universe) is neutral, bi-sexual or balanced. The left-hand Pillar is feminine and catalytic, while the right-hand is masculine and analytic. There is an overall rotation from bottom centre (10) through 8/5/3/1 and returning 1/2/4/7 to 10. This cycle turns upon the pivot of 6.

A second rotation is found between left and right (2-3/4-5/7-8) while a third rotation is found between the Crown and the Kingdom or Being and Matter. These three conceptual rotations lock together to form the overall Sphere of Being.

The divisions and rotations are immensely valuable subjects for mediation upon polarity and harmonic phases of reality in truth. The fusion and interaction of the Spheres forms the connections known as Paths.

within living matter. Traditionally the faery realm is lit by stars, but not by Sun or Moon. This is because the faery realm, inherent within the body of the planet, is shielded from the powers of the Solar Being (Sun, Moon, and planets), yet open to the stellar powers. This shielding is a power of the archangelic being Auriel, who holds the Shield or Mirror of Earth. Auriel in the Heavens is mirrored by Lucifer in the Earth, the archangel embodied within the planet during an early cycle of evolution.

The old Celtic Church taught that Lucifer drew many angels with him when he fell into the Earth, long before humanity was formed. These became the faery races, the angels of the Mother Below. Out of the interaction of Lucifer and the planetary body many life forms were generated, the living creatures of our lands and seas, from the most minute to the most immense, the microbe to the whale. The faery races, however, were immortal. Humanity appeared as a third wave of being, the most recent to come into consciousness upon and within the Earth, mediating between the stars above and the stars below.

This tradition of 'Lucifer' is nothing to do with evil or the propagandised 'devil'. The name of the morning star has become attached to a pre-Christian tradition about light within the Earth, within sacred living matter. Many of the deeper teachings and realisations of the faery tradition or the Underworld involve passing beyond the propaganda often embedded in folklore, and discovering the mystery of Earth Light, Lucifer, the Lux Mundi, the androgynous consciousness of universal being within the planet.

To conclude this chapter, we have a teaching or communication from one of the faery sources:-

THE THREEFOLD ALLIANCE OR THE PERFECTION OF LUCIFER

One of the operations (of the Faery and Underworld tradition) has become known as the Perfection of Lucifer. It is found in the reuniting of that which has become separate. Here is a key to it.

Three orders of being live within the world (within and not upon, for nothing that lives is of the surface only). They are the human races, the faery races, and the races of creatures within the land, sea, and air. (Angelic and other spiritual beings that may be known and unknown are not within the world as humans, faeries and creatures, though they may have exchanges with the three orders and be in worlds adjoining).

All three orders are of one another, yet many do not know it and cause suffering to themselves and others through their ignorance. At the original moment of the Bright One (Lucifer) embodied in the Earth these three, once united, were separated out to walk different ways through time, place, and power. They seem to have appeared in the world at times vastly removed from one another as if in three separate appearances, but this is due to the mystery of original embodiment and its triple power.

The faery races (of which there are many in each land) were of the original perfect world unmanifest, and retained its starry light when they entered into the Earth. The races of creatures which appeared next in land sea and air, were of the increasingly manifest and less perfect world, yet innocent. Human races, which appeared last, were of the potentially balanced world, found through knowledge, but because the triple power of separation is reflected in a small way in each of them, they are prone to forget. (This balanced world of humanity was to be at the threshold and able to cross back and forward at will. Such knowledge is still available, though it is more of an art than a science).

Through unity of the three orders of being, Human, Faery and Animal Animal, the Sleeper in the Land is awakened. This is the way of perfection that is so hidden as a truth that few know of it. The awakening of the Bright One, Lucifer, is not of the Land alone, but of the whole world. It is the light of the world shining back to the Sun which is its sister, and each knowing that they are of the stars and united in being.

Three utterances of light from the Mother Dark. The first gave substance to the Bright One, who was both male and female. This giving of substance is what is now called the Fall of Lucifer, and when the star fell the faery races also fell into the body of the Earth. (To the old ones there was no hint of pride or sin in this fall, for these follies are only human and the stars do not sin). At this utterance the faery races had bodies of changeable light, and all other forms were mirrored in these.

The second utterance made substance of the human races, and this is what is now called the creation and fall of Adam and Eve and the expulsion from Paradise. (And all such imputations of division through Woman and temptation are wrong, for as the old stories tell us, Woman is the guardian of the way to our true home and not the cause of any fall through sin).

Between the first and second utterance, which are the separations of the faery and human races from their stellar union, the five zones (of power in the body of the Earth) lived and moved and made the lands and seas. Out of this movement emerged all the living creatures, and those with faces moved outwards and those without faces moved inwards living upon and within the others. And all beings live as movements out of and into the substance of the Earth and partake of one another.

So the creatures are constantly moving between the faery realms and the realms of mortals, the lands above and below. They aspire towards the knowledge and companionship of man and woman, and yet return to the first and primal world of innocence. And this spiritual movement of the creatures is mirrored in their seasonal passage from place to place. They may still go where mortals are unable to reach, and so the seers and walkers go with them and come back again.

The Third Utterance

The third utterance is of the spirit of regeneration, which has many names, but is known to you as the redeemer and as Christ. The power of this utterance passed not into the land but into the entire world, seeking to pass through the Second Utterance and further in to merge with the First.

When the human faery and creature races recognise one another and come together again, the Redeemer will have completed gestation within the body of the planet. There is a Fourth Utterance, which for the world is yet to come, and this is the fourth of the great winds of the stars. This utterance transforms the world into a being of perfect manifest knowledge and open mind (to have no memory but being perfect in present knowledge of all that was past or future). This is the Mystery of the rebirth of Christ as Woman, during the last age of the world.

How shall you come to this wonder, sleeping within the earth yet awake among the stars? When you knock upon the door of the realms within the Land, you meet first the prophets and ancestors who have passed within, such as Merlin and the rest. And when you are able to pass through the realms, you will find the Sleepers of each land and of each of the Five Zones. Every location will have its way to the Sleepers, but you must seek ever further in and in.

At the heart of the realms, the heart of the world, is the perfect light of regeneration. This is the united power of the First and Third Utterances, and this too sleeps but for brief awakenings. This Sleeper at the Heart of the World awaits the acknowledgement of the Second Utterance, which is to say the union of all three orders of being within the world. Now you may come to this union and make acknowledgement through intent, through the way of passing within the Land and through the realms.

But the union also comes of itself, for the light will emerge and the Sleeper awaken when the period of nurture in the womb of the Earth is complete.

Do not assume, therefore, that you are barred from the light, for if you enter into the power within the Land, you will come to the power of the Earth itself. When you enter the power of the Earth, you will come to the light and to knowledge and memory. Whatever is of the world is echoed within you – the three utterances are there, and when you unite with the co-walkers of the other orders, faery and creature, the Fourth Utterance will arise from within the Earth and within yourself, speaking at once for both.

Sacrifice

What do you sacrifice to Her but your presumed fall? When She destroys you she consumes your fall from grace, She withdraws this aspect of yourself into her Body which is grace itself, for the Earth is a mirror that changes whatever is reflected within it. She will cause you to be reborn in a new form, just as the redeeming power of Christ will be reborn in a new form. And if you enter into the power of the Land and of the Earth itself, you will find that the rebirth has already come, and only your own separation and forgetfulness keeps you from it and from knowledge of it.

The Three Strains

Do not assume that we are talking only of three strains, qualities or types within yourself. Admittedly all three, the human, faery, and creature strains are echoed in you, and how could this not be so, for the three Utterances are in you. So you mirror the ages of the world.

We are not discussing a merging or assimilation of three appetites, three behaviours, or three classes of mind and emotion, though you may draw many such threads together, and rightly. We mean this: three distinct orders of being, human, faery, and creatures, that may unite to reunite. These are the three strains of our way, the three orders that partake of it. There are others also, who join with us, but for you the three strains must come first.

When the three emerged as distinct entities in a new world, which is a new time and space, the faery race had nothing of humanity in it. The creatures that afterwards generated out of the lands and seas had something of the faery powers, which are of the perfect world, and a little of humanity, such as the possibility of love and partnership. Humanity, coming out of the stars but becoming of the Earth, has all three strains within, but has excluded itself from knowledge of the other two.

This exclusion may seem to you to be through the pursuit of knowledge of matter, as if the one type of knowledge bars the other, but it is the effect of the power of isolation and materialisation. These are the great mirroring powers that we use to bring change speedily through intent, rather than to be changed slowly and unwittingly. Place a mirror to a mirror and see for yourself. Do you see what animal you have within that you have forgotten, and what animals without are your own partners? What faery blood and tribe shows in your face and form when you look in the glass, and which of the faery hives will appoint co-walkers to you ?

Within man and woman the balance of the Four Elements may be found in potential, though it is seldom realised. One way that was long hidden from the oppressors was the marriage of human and faery races, which brings a sexual union and, for the human, weaves the soul and ties it to the faery race for millennia. Beyond that is the Triune being, which is not a marriage, for there is no sexual union, but an intentional triple bond between human, faery, and creature. This is an equal and balanced partnership, leading to a revelation.

While the human races have all Four Elements and one or more of these weak, the faery beings have either triple or single Elements, while the creatures have double. Thus the Triune alliance may have Seven or Nine patterns of reiteration: it may pass through all worlds, and none may bar its way.

Thomas Rhymer, and
the Song of Smallness

The First

The first he was a gardener
    The first to dig in ground
    The second was a shepherd boy,
    He was this gardener's son.

The third he was a hunting man
    Who hunted with his horn,
    And with a bloody butcher's knife
    He's laid his brother down.

How bitterly his blood calls out
    How bitter is the sound,
    And if you seek to comfort him,
    He waits beneath the ground.

The first she is the Opener
    The opener of night,
    The second is the Gatherer
    Who holds the stars from flight.

The third he is the Shining One
    The brightest of them all,
    Who loved the dark and waiting Earth
    And into her did fall.

How constantly his voice calls out
    From deep within a stone,
    And if you seek to greet the dawn,
    You wait all night alone.

Each letter of his name is woven
    In a cloak of Song,
    And those who wove it long ago
    They danced when it was done.

R J Stewart 1978

Thomas Rhymer, and The Song Of Smallness

The Vision and Journey of Thomas Rhymer

Of the small number of faery ballads preserved in oral tradition, two are particularly powerful and important as initiatory visions. The first is Tam Lin in which a girl redeems her lover from the Underworld and the Dark Queen; the second is Thomas Rhymer in which a journey through the faery realm is described. (I have discussed both of these ballads in detail in *The Underworld Initiation* and other books; a story based on Thomas Rhymer is found in *Legendary Britain*, and a story based on Tam Lin in *Celtic Myths, Celtic Legends*).

The vision of Thomas Rhymer is a major oral source of faery initiatory lore. As a ballad it was sung for centuries, and still exists in oral tradition in Scotland today. Thomas Rhymer or Thomas of Erceldoune (Earslton) lived in 13th century Scotland. He was famous as a seer, with various vernacular prophecies attributed to him, the early prose Tristan, and a long Romance poem of his journey to Elfland or the faery realm. But the oral tradition preserved a simple stark ballad, which if we presume its origins to be 13th century, was preserved for seven hundred years by oral transmission. It may be that the vision itself is far older than its historical location, for the tradition can be traced back in various sources and legends of the Underworld or Otherworld, and in the myth of the Sacred Apple and the goddess.

The Ballad of Thomas Rhymer (Note: in this text some of the Scottish dialect words have been Anglicized for the general reader. Detailed texts in the Scottish vernacular are found in F.J.Child's collection *The English and Scottish Ballads*.)

1
True Thomas lay on a grassy bank,
And He beheld a lady gay,
A lady that was brisk and bold,
To come riding o'er the ferny brae.

2
Her skirt was of the grass-green silk,
Her mantle of the velvet fine,
And on every lock of her horse's mane,
Hung fifty silver bells and nine.

3
True Thomas he took off his hat,
And bowed low down to his knee,

"All hail thou virgin, Queen of Heaven,
For your like on Earth I ne'er did see."

4
"Oh no, oh no True Thomas " she said,
"That name does not belong to me;
I am but the Queen of Fair Elfland
That has come for to visit here with thee"

5
"And you must go with me now,Thomas,
True Thomas you must go with me,
And you must serve me seven years,
Through good or ill as may chance to be"

6
She turned about her milk white steed
And took True Thomas up behind,
And aye whene'er the bridle rang,
The steed flew faster than the wind.

7
For forty days and forty nights
They wade through red blood to the knee,
And he saw neither sun nor moon,
But heard the roaring of the sea.

8
Oh they rode on and further on,
Until they came to a garden tree,
"Light down, light down, you lady fair,
And I'll pull of that fruit for thee"

9
"Oh no, Oh no True Thomas " she says,
"That fruit may not be touched by thee,
For all the plagues that are in hell
Are upon the fruit of this country"

10
"But I have bread here in my lap,
Likewise a bottle of red wine,
And before that we go further on,
We shall rest, and you may dine."

11

When he had eaten and drunk his fill,
She said "Lay you head down on my knee,
And before we climb yon high high hill,
I will show you wonders three."

12

"Oh do you see that broad broad road
That lies by the lily leven?
Oh that is the road of wickedness,
Though some call it the road to Heaven"

13

And do you see that narrow narrow road
All beset with thorns and briars?
Oh that is the way of righteousness,
Though after it few enquires."

14

And do you see that bonny bonny road
Which winds about the ferny brae?
Oh that is the road to Fair Elfland,
And together there you and I will go"

15

"But Thomas you must hold your tongue
Whatever you may hear or see...
For if one word you chance to speak,
You will never get back to your own country."

16

And he has gotten a coat of woven cloth,
Likewise the shoes of velvet green,
And till seven years were past and gone,
  True Thomas ne'er on earth was seen.

If we summarise the narrative we find the following stages:

1   Sleeping under a sacred tree, the Hawthorn
2   Meeting the faery Queen
3   Travelling with her into the Underworld
4   Wading through rivers of blood (sometimes of blood and tears)
5   Absence of Sun and Moon, but sound of roaring sea
6   Vision of Garden and Apple tree
7   Warning concerning the fruit

8   Fruit is transformed as bread and wine
9   Vision of Three Roads: Wickedness, Righteousness, Elfland.
10 Service in Elfland, with gifts of green coat and shoes and the tongue that
     cannot lie.
11 Return to human world.

This vision is a classic source of how to conduct an Underworld experience, go there and back again. It also contains many of the power-keys to the Underworld and faery initiations: the Dark Queen or goddess, the land within the earth, the sacred Apple Tree (conferring either madness or immortality), a ritual of transubstantiation, changing one deadly substance into another nourishing substance, the vision of three possible roads, and finally the gifts. The green coat and shoes are traditionally associated with the vitality of the land, while the tongue that cannot lie is the gift of truth-speech or prophecy.

For those who like to explore themes, motifs and parallels, our next tale is based, in part, upon the worldwide tradition of people who step entire into other planes of existence. Every year thousands of people vanish. This is documented fact in our information-obsessed culture; for centuries there have been stories concerning those who vanish into other dimensions, Faeryland, strange worlds, mysterious realms. Many of the primal initiatory or magical arts are based firmly upon contact with such worlds or dimensions, and upon being able to enter into them. There is an enduring tradition in Scotland, as in other parts of Europe, concerning people who vanish into the Faery realm and meet with the inhabitants therein. This is supposed to have happened to certain historical persons, such as the thirteenth century poet Thomas the Rhymer, and the seventeenth century clergyman Robert Kirk.

Of course, there are other ways to interpret this tale, such as the seeming conflict between the inner life of the imagination and the outer life of daily work and duty, but we need not indulge in too many rational explanations. The Song of Smallness, both the tale and its originating song, also contain a number of what might be termed magical technicalities or rules and methods of working magic; I leave it to the reader to ferret these out.

The Song of Smallness (a faery tale)

Every evening she would listen for the voice, just as light and darkness merged together. At first there would be a spattering of rain upon window glass, then a gust of wind through the susurrating poplars. If she listened too hard the sound would be lost amid her straining; but in the slap of the stream beyond the garden, the last call of evening birds, she knew that the voice was singing. Singing to her.

Inside the house was a bright warmth of lamps, heat from the stove, a kettle that bubbled and gurgled occasionally. All the toys and blue plates of small ambition, human levels too low for her wild outreaching. When she had first come here she had wanted to smash the glass, stamp upon the crocks, hurl the heavy pans out of their smug hanging places over the stove. In time her violence had faded, urged inwards towards a more potent centre of discontent. Indeed, she kept the house immaculate, as if the height of her despising lay in pretence of acceptance.

One evening as spring rain poured unceasingly, she sat in an upstairs room, watching light change over the water meadows. As clear long grey light clarified the trees, she heard the voice. First the drops of heavy rainfall ceasing, then a whisper among branches far away. It seemed as if the voice was suddenly close, yet more distant than the clouds.

> "Small am I beneath your window,
> *Small am I hear me sing,*
> While you watch some distant road turning,
> *Oh the wind and rain*".

These words were woven into a high deep melody that swooped and fell, a leaf sliding through her mind at sunset. Instantly it was over, but she sat waiting and watching until total darkness surrounded the house.

Weeks passed before it came again, weeks of daily cleaning, cooking, tending. Caring without caring. She would find herself listening, hardly remembering what for, then suddenly resume her task, her pose. One evening while alone in the warm house, she heard it sing again. A water bird croaked across a dark river, a bat flew beyond the glass of the window, wind slid through the loose frame to stroke her cheek.

> "Voice of birdsong, touch of leaf fall,
> *Small am I, hear me sing,*
> While you tend the mill of earth call,
> *Oh the wind and rain.*"

Days become less tolerable after this second visitation. She became more bright and cheerful, more neighbourly than ever. People commented on how she had come out of herself. She had never, in truth, been so far within as she was at that time. Faces, voices, plans, hopes, flurried past her, meaningless phantoms of dream people. Hands held, plates clashed, forks and knives washed and wiped. Outer time seemed to accelerate to headlong speed; sunup and sunset merged into one hot glow all false division melted through. The dream people, those who lived out of themselves, did not see this.

Each evening she would go into the upper room and watch for the long clear light that could be felt even under cloud shadows. Waiting for the song to continue.

> "Light my hand upon your forehead,
> *Small am I hear me sing,*
> While you lie still in your shadow bed,
> *Oh the wind and rain.*"

By summer the haunting light came late. She took long walks alone in the meadows; cows bellowed, ducks laughed, green and gold life breathed upon her. The poplars danced full leaved endless rhythms of a distant sea, and she would return to the house by sunset. Not once did she stay out in the open for the voice, it was as if she knew that it could come to her only through a veil. Human window glass, ephemeral stone walls. No direct contact was possible at that time.

By autumn, as the first grain was harvesting, she heard another verse:

> "While the Moon turns, while the Stars crawl,
> *Small am I hear me sing,*
> Down the threads within the Lady's shawl,
> *Oh the wind and rain.*"

Now the season drew in towards short daylight. There was less time to see off the games, shams, toys of daily life before her evening ritual of listening and waiting. None of the dream people seem concerned to disturb her window sitting, so out of time and place that it hardly seemed to happen. They could not see it.

The leaves blew in great clouds and swirls across the river full of heavy brown water. Pools grew in the meadow, long trails of birds had flown to other lands. She longed now for another verse, feeling that the song was almost complete. The last verse, she knew, would arrive when the last leaf had fallen or the first ice skin wrinkled across the pools.

In the house the stove burned constantly. Thick stone walls grew warm slowly, buttresses against the coming force of cold. The last verse came very late, as stars burst out of the blue-black sky. Her breath made mist upon the glass as she leaned forward to listen:

> "Small am I to gain all openings,
> *Small am I, hear me sing,*
> In full time and tide I touch all things,
> *Oh the wind and rain... *"

By morning a thick dense snow had fallen, with clouds driving up out of the east suddenly. All shapes upon the ground were levelled into a smooth white mirror for the hard day. As the first distant shouts and laughter of children pulling sledges echoed across the water, a few of the dream people came up from the kitchen. They looked into her room, wondering where she might be.

Diving Through the
Moon Pool

Some Basic Exercises

There are a variety of what might be called full-scale visualisations and energy aligning techniques that enhance our awareness of the Underworld. These elaborate narratives, originally preserved in oral tradition, and, in the ancient cultures, temple training, also bring us into direct interaction with Underworld energies and entities. Both the traditional and modern forms, such as those in this book, prepared from my own individual experience and from group work, bring transformation within ourselves, and eventually enable mediation of the light within the earth.

Our role as humans is, or ought to be, as mediators, as bridges between the worlds, bringing certain modes of consciousness and energy to other life forms that are separated to a greater or lesser degree. At present it seems that most of the separation is our own, we have cut ourselves off from all other forms of life and consciousness, including our own planet and our fellow beings upon it and within it.

I would recommend finding a balance between the visualised imaginative techniques, such as the narrative journeys (part of a venerable collective tradition) and the direct energy techniques, such as those which follow shortly. For most people, but not all, it is creative and repeated work with imagery, narratives, visualisation, that awakens and realigns the energies. Other methods are ritual pattern-making, movement, silent meditation, and sink-or-swim encounter techniques such as those found in primal or chthonic magic. After this awakening has occurred, and this is the initiation, the more direct techniques can be used at will.

The potent force of the imagination frees up our energy patterns, and if we use traditional initiatory techniques, gives us a framework of images that holds great potential for inner transformation. The same potent force can be used to degrade and enervate ourselves...it is all, as an isolated materialist might say unwittingly, in the imagination.

We literally image what we are. Through rampant greed, indifference and materialism we have imaged ourselves into increasing antagonistic isolation; we reject all other orders of life, abuse them, deny their very existence. Then we wonder why humanity feels alone in the universe, why we turn upon one another in misery, rage, and anguish. If we use our imagination to open ourselves out of our isolation, we find that the world is full of many beings, many realities. The world is not simply our planet, but the total environment, the universal world. In and of this universal world, is our very substance, matter, the body. It is both our body, renewed daily out of the substance of the land, and the planetary body, with its different zones, continents, lands, and power-places.

If we work with the light within the land, the energy inherent in the faery realm Underworld within and beneath our conscious interpretation of our environment, remarkable changes occur.

Let us look at some simple exercises that enhance this interaction with the Underworld and its energies. In these exercises we are concentrating primarily upon energies rather than entities...the visualisations and traditional imagery give form to the beings, just as our own beings are given form through the collective image of humanity upon the land. These exercises have been developed in my own work over a period of fifteen years or more and I have designed them for general use by modern individuals and groups. There is another related set of older techniques embodied within various traditions which have the same effect, but are often confusing or inaccessible to the modern mind.

The Rising Light Below

This is a simple but major technique for arousing energy and passing it through your body: the power that rises from the Underworld, the Light within the Earth, will awaken and transform your own energies far more effectively than concentrating in isolation upon your power centres or chakras. If you do this exercise once every day, and also work with visualisation techniques on a regular basis, you will realign and activate your own energy centres rapidly.

This exercise is the mirror-working to those well publicised techniques which call down light 'from above'. In both cases the energy seems to begin outside the individual (though this understanding changes as you develop your inner powers), but in this technique the light is inherent within the Underworld, often in a latent mode. Human awareness activates the power, and draws it up through the body of the land into the human body. The Rising Light Below exercise is most effective while standing, though it may also be done sitting cross-legged, as squatting and cross-legged postures all enhance our earth-contact. Here are the stages, with some brief notes on their development and effect:

1   *Begin with a period of silence and steady regular breathing.* Your arms are lowered, with the finger tips stretched and pointing towards the ground. If you are sitting they may touch the ground lightly or rest upon your thighs. This initial arm position is important, as you will be raising your arms to different positions through the exercise.

2   *Be aware of the point of contact between your body and the ground.* If this is the floor of a room be aware that the building is in contact with the ground, with the land. For obvious reasons this type of exercise is

enhanced by working directly upon the surface of the land, or in a cave, basement, or underground chamber. By the holism, paradox, or 'law' of reflections and octaves, it also works very well in high places, such as the tops of hills and in tall buildings. Many Underworld techniques are useful for those of us who live in a city environment, as they pass directly through the imbalanced enervating city energy-field, which has little or no effect upon them. If you live in an unhealthy energy-isolated building, do this exercise on the roof or in the basement as well as in your own apartment.

3 *Visualise a source of energy just below the ground or floor where your feet or body makes contact.* This is usually felt and seen as a glowing ball of light. The upper surface of this energy-sphere touches the soles of your feet (or your legs, thighs, and buttocks if you are sitting in a cross-legged position), and from its lower surface a strand of light descends into the heart of the land, into the depths of the planet to an unknown source. This is your reflected energy field in the Underworld, normally latent. You are going to activate it, bring it alive through conscious work. Remember that it is part of you, reflected energy which you do not normally access or use, something of which millions of people are completely unaware, even those who practice meditation and energy techniques.

4 *Increase your awareness of this energy sphere: feel it touching you, move your imagination into it.* You may feel your personal energies descending into it, and a sensation of heat where your body touches the ground.

5 *Gradually draw the energy source into yourself.* This is done by breathing steadily, and feeling the energy sphere rise through your feet into your body. Your arm/hand position is slowly raised, drawing the energy with it. There are four zones of the body/energy field: FEET/GENITALS/HEART/THROAT (HEAD). (see figure 3). These are our human reflections of the holism of the Elements and Worlds.(See figures 1 and 2).

6 *FEET: be aware of the Element of Earth, and the matter or substance of your entire body.* The energy sphere rises up through your feet legs and thighs. This is the first awakening of energy within your physical substance. Your arms are still directed downwards, but slowly raised, drawing the energy as they move.

7 *GENITALS: be aware of the Element of Water, and the twofold nature of water in your body.* Firstly it is the fundamental element of your cells; on a non-physical level Water is the element of creation, birth, sexual union, love, and represents the second awakening of energy within your physical substance. Your arms are raised gradually to waist height.

8   *HEART: be aware of the Element of Fire*. As the energy sphere rises, it gradually becomes more incandescent. The Four Elements are simultaneously literal and metaphysical. At this heart level the increasing rate of your energy becomes fire. In your body this is bio- electrical energy, the flow of blood, and the subtle forces that radiate from your life core. As these subtle forces manifest they appear in an increasingly watery and earthy form. The incandescence of the energy sphere rising from the Underworld through your body is the third awakening of energy within your physical substance. Your arms are raised, palms upward, to shoulder height.

9   *THROAT (Head): be aware of the Element of Air*. The energy has now risen to surround your head and shoulders (see figure 3), and has reached its most rapid and mobile rate. All Four Zones are now alive, each rising level through the body being holistically within one another. Yet the elevation of energy towards the head causes an increase in rate, and changes of our consciousness. Your arms are raised above the head, palms upwards.

10 *Returning the power*. Simply reverse the sequence by steadily lowering your arms, and feeling the power pass down through your body. It returns steadily to your energy sphere within the land, below your feet. As it descends, you lower your arms, and each of the Four Zones gently reduces in activity.

Meditation within this technique. As this is an energy arousal technique, you need not pause and meditate within it at all. Meditation, however, will greatly enhance the effect, and will put you into conscious awareness of the energies in and through your body. Pausing for meditation works best after you have developed the raising and lowering technique in its own right. In other words, do not use this exercise and begin to meditate upon each of the four Zones in depth before you have completed the full cycle several times.

You may meditate upon each Zone as it rises, or as it descends. As this involves arm movement, remember that you will feel tension in your arms and body. These tensions were used in ancient temple training as sources of power, and the arm positions have a strong effect upon the flow of energy through your body.

AN ESSENTIAL NOTE When you raise the energy sphere to the Throat/Head zone, hold it there. This is the most ecstatic zone in terms of meditation, and there is often a tendency to lose some of the simple control. Your arm position, and the tension of it, serve to keep the energy field in the head-zone. You should not move into any predefined awareness, imagery, or any other means by which the energy sphere

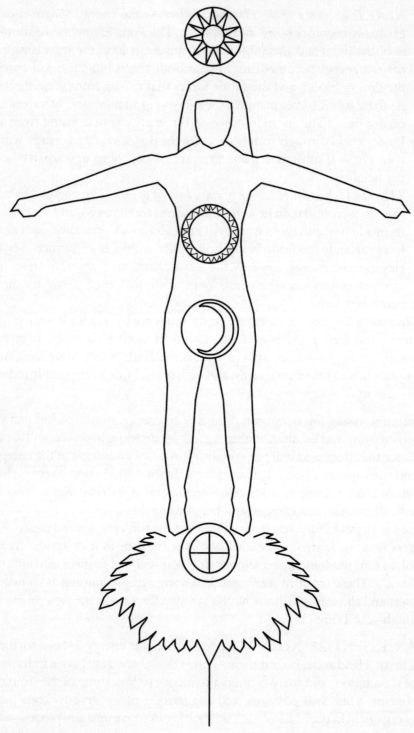

Figure 3 The Four Zones

may rise away above your head and disperses. Remember you are drawing the subtle force of the Underworld, and of your own being reflected in that realm, and not making an offering or seeking to share or disperse your energy as you might in religious devotion or sexual ecstasy.

You may feel an ecstatic sense of union, have visions of stars, and most of all, a response from the light above which is the consciousness of our sun as a spiritual being. If you do experience this, (and though many people do, not everybody does) do not rush off into it, as you will simply lose your energy. Always aim to pass the power back through your body: anything that is harmonised from the Direction of Above will flow with your intent, and pass through you into the land.

So little conscious work is done today with the land and the Underworld realms, that circulating energy in this way is an essential work of sharing, transformation, and affirmation of the spirit inherent in matter.

When your energy sphere is returned to the latent position, reflecting just below the ground, you will find that your awareness of the land, the natural world, and of many subtle energies and beings is enhanced. Finally, as always, make some brief notes.

The next stage of this energy working is to pass energy in and out of specific locations, objects, and other life-forms, such as plants and trees.

Diving Through The Moon Pool

This exercise is based upon an old traditional technique known as Diving through the Moon, or Moon Pool which is described here in three variant forms. Each has its advantages, and we begin with a basic version using a tarot trump or other suitable picture image. Next comes an advanced version, in which a physical location or sacred site is used. The third variant is the original teaching from which the others have been adapted. This original teaching is a powerful example of techniques taught through direct Underworld contact, and should not be attempted literally without experience, skill, and understanding of its implications.

The original Moon Pool teaching (variant three) makes no distinction between outer and inner worlds, physical and spiritual realms. Our basic exercise for contemporary use (variant one) relies on a protected or undisturbed period of visualisation, working entirely in the inner worlds. The advanced exercise for contemporary use (variant two) fuses inner and outer worlds, involving both vision and physical location, but still distinguishes between them. Although the third variant is the most powerful and is the original, we should work towards it through the other two, which give us a

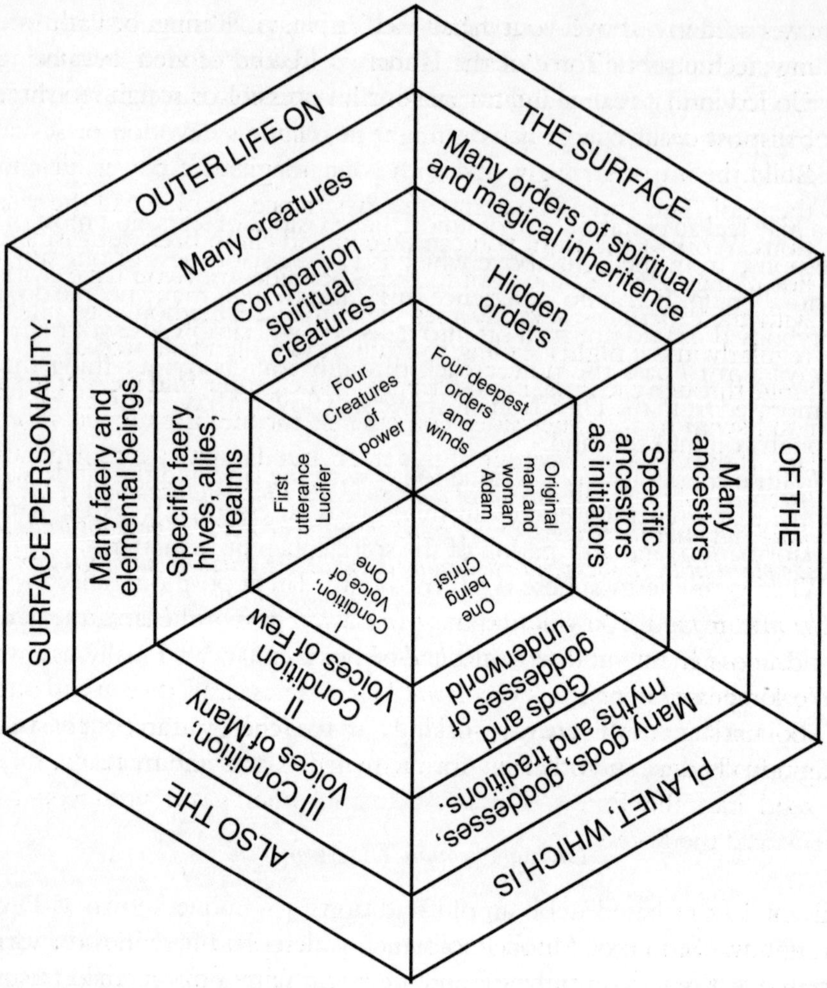
OUTER LIFE ON
THE SURFACE
OF THE
PLANET, WHICH IS
ALSO THE
SURFACE PERSONALITY.
Many creatures
Many orders of spiritual and magical inheritence
Many ancestors
Many gods, goddesses, myths and traditions.
III Condition: Voices of Many
Many faery and elemental beings
Companion spiritual creatures
Hidden orders
Specific ancestors as initiators
Gods and goddesses of underworld
II Condition Voices of Few
Specific faery hives, allies, realms
Four Creatures of power
Four deepest orders and winds
Original man and woman Adam
One being Christ
I Condition: Voice of One
First utterance Lucifer

Figure 4 Underworld Realms

gradual development and many safeguards against over-extending our awareness and energies.

(Variant One)

1 Begin with the Trump of The Moon from The Merlin Tarot or any other suitable tarot deck where this trump includes a pool. Become familiar with the image until you can see it clearly and steadily with your eyes closed. (If you are experienced in working with trumps, you should be aware that each trump has 'secret' paths and gates, which are not the

ones used in our well-established meditative, visualising, or Path-working techniques. The Merlin Tarot is recommended because the Underworld paths and gates are readily accessible through its trumps, but most decks will work).

2   Build the image strongly, and with your imaginative power, dive into the pool. This should be an intense experience, invoking all the sensations. Work at this until you can dive in and climb back out easily. Do not plunge through the pool to the other side until you have worked with the experience several times. An enhanced method is to practice regularly in the nights leading to a full moon, then take step 3.

3   Plunge through the Pool, diving deeply. Some people find it easier to dive in and swim to the other side. You emerge for the first time in another place. If the vision is uncertain at this stage, build it with your imaginative powers as follows: *you emerge at a cross- roads. One road leads out of the pool behind you, and three more are in front of you. The road to the right leads to a wide plain lit by flashes of Earth Light like wild fire darting out of the ground.*

The road to the left leads up to a steep mountain from which streams of water flow. The road before you leads to a wild dark forest.

Work repeatedly with this vision until it becomes clear: dive in and out of the Pool until the three roads are instantly visible when you arrive. The vision will gradually develop in detail with each visit. When you are ready, follow the road into the Forest. Do not take the other roads until you have experienced the Forest.

(Variant Two)
This an advanced version of the method, in which you choose any one of the three roads. See variant three for the direct teaching of this method from an Underworld contact (this is a very powerful technique which you should not try unless you are absolutely certain of your intent and willing to take total responsibility for your actions).

Advanced Method Of Working

Do not attempt this method until you are experienced in Underworld visualising and visions. Before you work with this you should have a good contact established with companion creatures and faery allies. The method seems simple but requires skill, stamina and the Threefold Alliance.

1   Become familiar with the visualisation of diving into the Moon Pool, through working with the trump of The Moon. You should have already experienced a range of Underworld and Faery contacts, and used the

Moon dive for admission to the Forest and witnessing the Sleeping Maiden.

2   Prepare yourself from the dark time of the Moon with meditation and daily stillness. On the full Moon find a reflective surface to work with. If you are working indoors you can use a mirror or bowl of water to reflect the moon. If possible find an actual pool or lake where you will not be disturbed.

3   Do not use any written or recorded source, but focus your awareness upon the reflection of the moon in the mirror or water. Use your power of vision to dive into it and emerge at the crossroads. Three roads are before you:

the road to the right leads to a wide plain lit by flashes of Earth Light like wild fire darting out of the ground.

the road to the left leads up to a steep mountain from which streams of water flow.

the road before you leads to the forest, but you are now able to make other meetings there or seek other contacts.

You can travel any or all of the three roads, though you would usually travel only one a month.

(Variant Three)

The Original Moon Pool Ceremony

(from an inner teaching contact)

Fast for three days before the full Moon. Remain chaste and clarify your sight ensuring that no shadows are in it. On the night of the full Moon go to the pool alone. Take with you a treasured possession to give to Her. (If the Moon is covered by clouds, stay for a time in silence and return home. Begin again with the next full Moon).

When you come to the pool look first at the Moon above. Circle the pool three times and acknowledge the power of the Four Winds. Sit with your gift and recall its story, then throw it far out into the pool. Watch the water until the ripples cease and you can see the mirrored Moon. When you see clearly, remove your clothing and dive naked into the pool.

Dive deep and swim swiftly to the other side. When you emerge you will be at the Crossroads. Choose a road and when you have chosen, a Guide will appear. Challenge the Guide if there is no speech or sign and only standing still. If the Guide challenges you, instantly answer with your first impulse and truth. If the Guide is hostile, call upon your co-walkers to appear, and the Guide will change form or be replaced by another. Do not threaten the

Guide or attempt any force. Your co-walkers will talk with the Guide for you if you cannot.

If no Guide appears, choose a road and walk it alone. Do not summon co-walkers, but reserve their aid for the return if necessary. Walk or run rapidly and fix the way in your mind avoiding all distraction. Do not leave the road until it ends. (Some hear calls of love or screams for help from the surrounding lands and see their loved ones or their enemies out of the corner of one eye. This is a false encounter from failing to clarify the vision and clouding the mind with low dreams during the three day fast. These false sounds and sights are from within yourself and take form briefly out of the power in the land. Do not follow them and they will cease).

In the place that you come to you will find your gift terribly changed. At first you may not know it, but by signs you will come to it. You must mould it into a new form by whatever means you can, summoning your skills. When that form is complete, One will come to you and destroy it with an Element. At this moment both destroyer and destroyed will vanish. At this moment you may meet Her. Be ready.

Return by whatever way to the pool, by the reverse road or another that is shown. When you reach the pool, dive in and swim to the other side. When you emerge, do not look at the sky. Wait watching the water until the ripples have ceased and you see the mirrored Moon. Now look up at the sky, dress, and return home.

The Four Visions

'At the time of their conquest, Dagda their high king made a distribution of all such palaces in his kingdom. He gave one sid to Lug, son of Ethne, another to Ogme; and for himself retained two – one called Brug na Boinne, or Castle of the Boyne, because it was situated on or near the River Boyne near Tara, and the other called Sid or Brug Maic ind Oc, which means Enchanted Palace or Castle of the Son of the Young. And this Mac ind Oc was Dagda's own son by the queen Boann, according to some accounts, so that as the name (Son of the Young) signifies, Dagda and Boann, both immortals, both Tuatha De Danann, were necessarily always young, never knowing the touch of disease, or decay, or old age. Not until Christianity gained its psychic triumph at Tara, through the magic of Patrick prevailing against the magic of the Druids – who seem to have stood at that time as mediators between the People of the goddess Dana and the pagan Irish – did the Tuatha De Danann lose their immortal youthfulness in the eyes of mortals and become subject to death. In the most ancient manuscripts of Ireland the pre-Christian doctrine of the immortality of the divine race 'persisted intact and without restraint'; but in the Senchus na relec or 'History of the Cemeteries', from the Leabhar na h-Uidhre, and in the Lebar gabala or 'Book of Conquests', from the Book of Leinster, it was completely changed by the Christian scribes.

When Dagda thus distributed the underground palaces, Mac ind Oc, or as he was otherwise called Oengus, was absent and hence forgotten. So when he returned, naturally he complained to his father, and the Brug na Boinne, the king's own residence, was ceded to him for a night and a day, but Oengus maintained that it was for ever. This palace was a most marvellous one: it contained three trees which always bore fruit, a vessel full of excellent drink, and two pigs – one alive and the other nicely cooked ready to eat at any time; and in this palace no one ever died. In the Colloquy, Caeilte tells of a mountain containing a fairy palace which no man save Finn and six companions, Caeilte being one of these, ever entered. The Fenians, while hunting, were led thither by a fairy woman who had changed her shape to that of a fawn in order to allure them; and the night being wild and snowy they were glad to take shelter therein. Beautiful damsels and their lovers were the inhabitants of the palace; in it there was music and abundance of food and drink; and on its floor stood a chair of crystal. In another fairy palace, the enchanted cave of Keshcorran, Conaran, son of Imidel, a chief of the Tuatha De Danann, had sway; 'and so soon as he perceived that the hounds' cry now sounded deviously, he bade his three daughters (that were full of sorcery) to go and take vengeance on one of our race if a fairy domain is violated. Frequently the fairy palace is under a lake, as in the christianized story of the Disappearance of Caenchomrac:- Once when 'the cleric chanted his psalm, he saw (come) towards him a tall man that emerged out of the loch: from the bottom of the water that is to say.' This tall man informed the cleric that he came from an underwater monastery, and explained 'that there should be subaqueous inhabiting by men is with God no harder than that they should dwell in any other place'. In all these ancient literary accounts of the Sidhe-palaces we easily recognize the same sort of palaces as those described to-day by Gaelic peasants as the habitations of the 'gentry', or 'good people', or 'people of peace'. Such habitations are in mountain caverns like those of Ben Bulbin or Knock Ma, or in fairy hills or knolls like the Fairy-Hill at Aberfoyle on which Robert Kirk is believed to heave been taken, or beneath lakes.

From *The Fairy Faith in Celtic Countries*,
W Y Evans Wentz, 1911

Hark to the tolling of bells
And the crying of wind!
The old spells
Time out of mind,
They are crying before me and behind!
I know now no more of my pain,
But am as the wandering rain
Or as the wind's shadow on the grass
Beyond Finias of the Dark Rose:
Or, 'mid the pinnacles and still snows
Of the silence of Falias,
I go: or am as the wave that idly flows
Where the pale weed in songless thickets grows
Over the towers and fallen palaces
Where the sea-city was,
The city of Murias.

Extract from *The Dirge of the Four Cities* by Fiona Macleod

In this chapter we explore the faery realm through four visions. As recommended earlier, read them through as stories several times before working with them. The four visions should be done separately, one at a time, and only combined when you have experience and stamina.

They are the 'four cities' or convokations of the faery realm, of the Irish Tuatha de Danaan, the immortals who appeared from another world into our own. In this tradition we find the earliest source for the ideas of the Sword, Rod, Cauldron, and Stone, in the directions East, South, West, and North.

Sacred Space, the Seven Directions, is a powerful key to work within the Underworld and the Fairy realm. The directions and the Elements of Air, Fire, Water, and Earth, act as a relative pattern for our energies and consciousness when we explore other worlds and interact with their inhabitants. In working with the fairy realm, the four directions of East, South, West, and North carry a wealth of associations, particularly as the primal land is attuned to the energies of the four directions.

This directional pattern of energy, zoning and harmonising the land, was a feature of ancient Celtic culture, and indeed of many cultures worldwide. It is still found inherent within our planetary directions today, and is not a theorised pattern, but a practical one based upon the polarity of the Earth and the movement of planet around the sun.

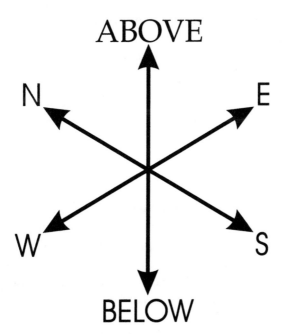

Figure 5   The Seven Directions

The associations of the Seasons and Elements with the Directions is, therefore, a holism within which a relative cycle of energy occurs. We may use this cycle of the directions and its seasonal and elemental energies in our visualisation of the fairy realm.

When we do so, we attune to the primal land, with its empowered directions, and simultaneously relate and attune the Elements and phases of consciousness (the Seasons) within ourselves. In many wisdom traditions involving transpersonal development, the Elements and related cycles, often called the Wheel of Life, form the basis of all meditation, visualisation, and ritual pattern making. When this holism is realised within the fairy realm, we find that it takes on characteristics of that realm, and also enables the powers of the fairy land, the primal land, to be realised and manifested for us, within us, and so through us towards the regeneration of our own world.

There are four cities that no mortal eye has seen but that the soul knows; these are Gorias, that is in the East; and Finias that is in the South; and Murias that is in the West; and Falias that is in the North. And the symbol of Falias is the stone of death, which is crowned with pale fire. And the symbol of Gorias is the dividing sword. And the symbol of Finias is a spear. And the symbol of Murias is a hollow that is filled with water and fading light'.
From *The Little Book of the Great Enchantment* (Fiona Macleod).

Wind comes from the spring star in the East; fire from the summer star in the South; water from the autumn star in the West; wisdom, silence, and death from the star in the North.'
From *The Divine Adventure* (Fiona Macleod)

Fiona Macleod (William Sharp, 1855–1905) used an obscure model of Four Cities in several poems. These are said to be the original dwellings of the Tuatha De Danann, and are listed in early Irish poetry. The concept is closely related to the ancient provinces of Ireland and the Four Implements or magical weapons of the Tuatha De Danann, the ancient Irish gods and goddesses who in later oral and written traditions become identified with the high fairy race.

The implements or Hallows are the Sword, Spear, Cup or cauldron, and Stone. We may use this directional pattern, and the four otherworldly 'cities' in visualisation, revealing the deeper mysteries of the fairy realm. If we explore the four primal cities or convocations of the fairy people, we enter the deepest levels of both fairy and ancestral knowledge and energy, for they are at the foundation of mythic awareness of the relationship between human and fairy realms.

The following visualisations should be done after working with the narrative vision of the Inverted Tree (see Chapter Two). They lead to deeper levels of the fairy realm, and connect to powerful forces within the sacred land.

Sacred Space is opened, and silence is realised

NOTE: Four meditational objects may be arranged upon a central small stand for these visualisations: they are (North) a quartz-veined stone; (West) a bowl of water; (South) a straight branch (pulled in one swift motion and not cut from the tree); and (East) a dagger or small sword of bronze or stone (not iron or steel).

THE OPENING VISION (to be used before each vision of the Four Directions).

We begin by building strongly in our inner vision the Four Directions of North, East, South, and West. In the North is night and winter; in the East is dawn and spring; in the South is noon and midsummer; in the West is autumn and evening.

As we build our vision of the Directions, we see the room in which we sit change into a square chamber, with a door in the wall of each Quarter, and know that we must pass through each door in turn to reach the four cities of the fairy realm: Gorias in the East, Finias in the South, Murias in the West, and Falias in the North.

EAST: First the door in the eastern wall opens, revealing a landscape beyond. We look upon the gateway of the east: it is in the form of two standing stones, with a narrow gap between them. Through this gap we see a spring landscape, lit by pale blue and green light.

SOUTH: Next the door in the southern wall opens, revealing a landscape beyond. We look upon the gateway of the South: it is in the form of two trees, one of green spreading branches and the other a tree of flame, constantly burning but never consumed. As we look upon these trees, they seem to exchange with one another; first one is flames then of green branches, then the other. We look between them and see a brilliantly lit land, with a distant hill rising directly in the centre of our line of sight.

WEST: Now the door in the western wall opens, revealing a landscape beyond. We look upon the gateway of the west: it is in the form of two low hills tinged with the light of evening. Beyond the hills is the sea, with a path of light stretching across it.

NORTH: Lastly the door in the northern wall opens, revealing the gateway of the north; it is in the form of a low thorn hedge, with a narrow gap in it. Beyond the gap we see a cave within a great wall of rock. Deep within the shadows of the cave we see a faint glow of silver-white light, like starlight.

One: The Vision of Gorias in the East

We will enter each of the Four Gates in turn, beginning with the gate of the East. From the East we feel a brisk wind, and hear faintly the sound of horns blowing. We step up to the two stones, and pass directly between them. Now we find ourselves upon a rolling grassy plain. The wind blows strongly in our face, and all round us long grass waves and ripples in the pale dawn-light. Looking for the source of the light, in the East ahead of us, we see a line of shapes silhouetted against the horizon, standing up out of the grass.

We feel drawn towards these shapes, and pause for a moment to dedicate our journey to the task of seeking and finding the mysterious city of Gorias, where the sacred sword of the Underworld is held.

Now we begin to walk forwards to the East, and as we step through the long grass our sight of the shapes upon the horizon becomes clear: we realise that we are walking towards a collection of standing stones. As we approach, we see an avenue of stones, with its entrance directly upon our path. It leads into a triple stone circle of single upright stones.

As we enter the avenue of stones, we see that the long grass grows right up to them, and it seems that the way has not been walked before us, for there is no track, no trampled grass. But when we look behind, we see that we have left no trail in the grass ourselves. We look back once more and see far away to the west two tiny upright stones amid the vast plain, marking the gate through which we entered.

Now we walk down the avenue of stones, and hear the wind seethe and mutter around them, and from the outermost ring of stone ahead of us a fluting sound rises and falls in long sliding tones. The wind plays its music upon the stones, and we wonder if this is the source of the sound of horns blowing that we heard before we entered the gateway of the East.

As we enter the outermost ring of stones, we realise that they are low, not much higher than the height of a man. Each stone is carved with spirals and shallow cup-marks, and we see that no stone is similar to any other. Each spiral, each hollow, conveys a wordless message to us, and we turn to the left, and walk around the circle, between the first and second row of stones. As we walk we each feel drawn towards one stone of the inner circle, and pause at that stone, wherever it may be. This is your stone companion, your life-stone in the East, and you commune with it in silence. (*Silent pause here*)

Now we emerge from our communion with the stones, and hear again the fluting sliding sound of the wind blowing...it seems now to come from the innermost circle of stones, and we look towards this. There are four huge rough stones with no carving upon them, and we step into the circle between the second and the innermost ring of stones. As we do so we feel a strong current flowing around the circle, as if we wade through deep water. The sound of the wind stops suddenly, and we enter the innermost circle in silence. It is empty.

As we look upon the circle of grass, in the silent light of perpetual dawn, we see the tip of a sword showing through the earth in the very centre of the circle. It has a polished green blade, and only a short length is visible. We stand around the circle, and feel the rough stones at our backs. It seems impossible to draw closer to the sword, as if the air resists us and the earth will not carry us. We long to know the mystery of the buried sword, rising up out of the earth, and meditate in silence upon it. *(Silent pause here)*

Over the sword we see now a shape forming, slowly, seeming to mould out of the air and light. It is the guardian of the mystery of Gorias, the city of the East. As this figure appears we are aware also of other presences in the stone circle, as if a great host has assembled invisibly while we have meditated upon the sword. One by one we approach the guardian, and seek the answer to a question. *(Pause here)*

Now we must return to the outer world, and leave the sacred sword, its guardian, and the city of the East. We slowly step out of the innermost circle, and as we do so the presence of the guardian and the invisible host instantly ceases; they vanish suddenly as if they had never been present. One by one we find our stones in the second circle, and feel the carvings on each stone, trying to understand its story, and why we were drawn to it when we entered.

Now we walk swiftly down the stone avenue, and out into the grassy plain. As we leave the outermost circle of stones, we hear the wind fluting and blowing behind us, in rising and falling sliding tones, like the blowing of unearthly horns. Once again we hear the sound of a great host gathering and murmuring in the stones, moving, whispering, crying sudden wild short cries. We know that we must not look back, but head resolutely for the gateway into the human world.

The two gate-stones are before us, and a huge wind rises at our backs and seems to blow us through. We pass between the stones, and find ourselves in a chamber with four doors. Here we pause and slowly return to our starting place, a familiar room in the human world. Gradually the image of the chamber with four doors dissolves, and we open our eyes to return to our outer awareness.

NOTE: At this point there should be a break, and an opportunity to write notes. Writing the contents of the visualisation out in a notebook often brings through material that might otherwise be forgotten. It is also useful for a group to discuss or share experiences after each of the Four Visions, but discussions should not be interpretative or psychological, as this will lessen the impact of the experience through attempting to rationalise it. Simple acceptance and writing of notes gradually builds into a body of understanding, symbols, and regular patterns of experience within the fairy realm. The experiences should always be accepted as themselves, not as analogues or allegories for something rationalised.

Two: The Vision of the City of Finias in the South

We begin by building strongly in our inner vision the Four Directions of North, East, South, and West. In the North is night and winter; in the East is dawn and spring; in the South is noon and midsummer; in the West is autumn and evening.

As we build our vision of the Directions, we see once again the room in which we sit change into a square chamber, with a door in the wall of each Quarter, and know that we must pass through each door in turn to reach the four cities of the fairy realm: Gorias in the East, Finias in the South, Murias in the West, and Falias in the North. We have already travelled to the city of Gorias in the East, and brought back with us keys to the power and meaning of that place. Now we will affirm each of the Cities in turn, and travel to the South.

EAST: First the door in the eastern wall opens, revealing a familiar sight beyond. We look upon the gateway of the east: it is in the form of two standing stones, with a narrow gap between them. Through this gap we see a spring landscape, lit by pale blue and green light. This is the realm of the EAST where the city of Gorias stands in perpetual dawn.

SOUTH: Next the door in the southern wall opens, revealing a landscape beyond. We look upon the gateway of the South: it is in the form of two trees, one of green spreading branches and the other a tree of flame, constantly burning but never consumed. As we look upon these trees, they seem to exchange with one another; first one is flames then of green branches, then the other. We look between them and see a brilliantly lit land, with a distant hill rising directly in the centre of our line of sight.

WEST: Now the door in the western wall opens, revealing a landscape beyond. We look upon the gateway of the west: it is in the form of two low hills tinged with the light of evening. Beyond the hills is the sea, with a path of light stretching across it.

NORTH: Lastly the door in the northern wall opens, revealing the gateway of the north; it is in the form of a low thorn hedge, with a narrow gap in it. Beyond the gap we see a cave within a great wall of rock. Deep within the shadows of the cave we see a faint glow of silver-white light, like starlight.

Our intention is to travel to the city of Finias, the white city of perpetual summer in the South. We focus our attention upon the door of the South, and stepping through it find ourselves before two tall trees, one of green leaves and branches, the other of brilliant orange, white, and red flames. As we look upon the trees, the image reverses, with the flames and green leaves interchanging. We feel a snap of energy pulsing through us as the image changes. To enter the summer land before us we must each step through the trees exactly as the pulse of energy changes from flames to green leaves.

he count the pulse of the transformations, and discover that it exchanges every nine heartbeats. On the ninth beat we step through, one by one. As we step through and the polarity of the trees exchanges, we feel a powerful surge of energy coursing through our bodies, and emerge into a brilliantly lit warm summery place.

The full light of a high summer noon fills this land, and the air is warm and rich with the scent of flowers. We hear the hum of bees, and feel the vibrancy of the plants around us. The landscape is rolling and filled with flowering plants, bushes, many aromatic herbs. Directly before us is a hill, and a faint trail wanders through the flowers towards it. The trail meanders and curves around small trees and clusters of flowering plants, and as we walk we feel the warmth of the land through our feet. The perfume of the plants is intoxicating, and as we walk the meandering path we feel exhilarated, and begin to see flashes of colour from the plants, as if a new level of sight, a new perception of light, has come to us.

Now the path divides into three, before a small flowering tree growing out of a cluster, a cairn, of coloured stones. The path to our left leads away through the rolling landscape towards a flat plain far in the distance. This side of the cairn is marked by green stones, and the road leads to Gorias by a way which we may not travel at this time.

The path to our right curves steeply away over the gentle hills and out of sight. This side of the cairn is made of blue stones, and the road leads to Murias by a way which we may not travel at this time. The path before us, just to the right of the flowering tree and cairn of coloured stones, leads to the hill. This is the way to the city of Finias which we must travel. The stones of this side of the cairn are white where the path passes. As we step forward we see that the stones facing north, the direction that we have come from, are black.

Before us the hill rises, and the path begins to spiral around it, gradually climbing to the top. The crown of the hill is wreathed in a white glowing cloud, through which we see tall dim shapes. As we slowly climb the hill, we see that there is a great circle of trees upon its summit, and that the white glowing cloud resolves itself into silver leaves and white blooms. Yet even as we look the sight dissolves again into a glowing white cloud. Climbing higher we look upon the land below, and see in the distant west the light shining upon the sea. In the distant east we see a flat plain and upon the horizon, an impossible distance away, the faint sight of upright stones. It is as if our vision is enhanced by the light of this place, and we can see for great distances, and perceive subtle colours and the very life essence of the trees and plants.

Now we reach the top of the hill, and find ourselves standing before a grove of tall slender trees. They are similar to poplar trees, but have silver-grey bark and white and pale green and silver leaves, with many white flowers. The trees sway back and forth gently, filling the air with a hissing sound and a faint but potent perfume. Within the centre of the grove the hilltop is flat, with closely cropped grass of a brilliant silvery green.

We pause here and affirm our intent to pass within and seek out the mystery of Finias, city of the South. *(Short silent pause here)*

Before we enter the grove we must walk around its perimeter, and as we do so we are each drawn to one of the trees. From the tree that you are drawn to, a being steps. This is your tree-companion in the South, and you may only step into the sacred grove with your companion. The tree-companion rests one hand upon your shoulders, and you commune in silence with one another. *(Silent pause here)*

The great trees sway and hiss as if there is a wind, yet we feel no breeze. The brilliant light shines like the sun at midsummer, hot and vital, yet there is no sun in the sky. With our companion beings, we step through into the sacred grove. Immediately the hissing sound increases until it fills the air, and we hear faint whispers, voices, sounds of movement all around us. We slowly walk around the perimeter of the grove, each guided by a companion, and look towards the centre. Where we had previously seen only grass, there now appears a white staff, set upright in the ground. We approach it slowly, and see that it has green buds as if it is about to break into leaf. Yet it is marked with a spiralling pattern, as if it is both crafted and living at the same time. As we move towards the centre of the circle, the noise around us stills, and there is a powerful feeling of expectancy, of being watched, of waiting for a wonder.

Now we stand before this living staff, and about it a cloudy shape appears. This is the guardian of the mystery of the staff, and we commune with this being in silence. *(Silent meditation here, music if possible)*

To each of us the guardian gives a gift, which we look upon and keep safe. Now our tree-companions bid us leave the sacred grove, and gently turn us around, each one guiding us towards the tree that has chosen us. As we reach the trees we hear a great sound of murmuring conversation and the music of harps, high singing tones are uttered, and many voices merge in a strange harmony. Our companions make it clear that we must not turn and look back, but push us out of the tree circle towards the path that leads down the hill.

Upon the summit of the hill of the South, the white City of Finias, we look again to the East and to the West, and now look for the first time to the North. The path spirals down the hill, and we see it leading away across the rolling countryside towards a gate of roaring flames, and beyond that gate we see blackness. This is the way that we must travel back to the human world.

Our descent of the hill is rapid, and we reach the dividing of the ways. From out of the little flowering tree a voice whispers one word to each of us, and we pause to remember what is said. *(Pause here)*

Now we make our way to the gateway, and the image of roaring flames resolves into two trees, each alternating flames and green leaves at great speed. As we approach we lose our exalted sight and sense of ecstasy that has filled us in the summer land, and the rate of interchange between the trees slows until it reaches one change every nine heartbeats. One by one we step through into the blackness beyond, and emerge into a plain chamber with four doors. The door behind us closes, and we dissolve the vision of the chamber, returning to a familiar room, and ready to emerge into the outer world of human life.

Three: The Vision of Murias in the West

We begin by building strongly in our inner vision the Four Directions of North, East, South, and West. In the North is night and winter; in the East is dawn and spring; in the South is noon and midsummer; in the West is autumn and evening.

As we build our vision of the Directions, we see once again the room in which we sit change into a square chamber, with a door in the wall of each Quarter, and know that we must pass through each door in turn to reach the four cities of the fairy realm: Gorias in the East, Finias in the South, Murias in the West, and Falias in the North. We have already travelled to the cities of Gorias in the East and Finias in the South, and brought back with us keys to the power and meaning of those places. Now we will affirm each of the Cities in turn, and travel to the West.

EAST: First the door in the eastern wall opens, revealing a familiar sight beyond. We look upon the gateway of the east: it is in the form of two standing stones, with a narrow gap between them. Through this gap we see a spring landscape, lit by pale blue and green light. This is the realm of the EAST where the city of Gorias stands in perpetual dawn.

SOUTH: Next the door in the southern wall opens, revealing a familiar landscape beyond. We look upon the gateway of the South: it is in the form of two trees, one of green spreading branches and the other a tree of flame, constantly burning but never consumed. As we look upon these trees, they seem to exchange with one another; first one is flames then of green branches, then the other. We look between them and see a brilliantly lit land, with a distant hill rising directly in the centre of our line of sight.

WEST: Now the door in the western wall opens, revealing a landscape beyond. We look upon the gateway of the west: it is in the form of two low hills tinged with the light of evening. Beyond the hills is the sea, with a path of light stretching across it.

NORTH: Lastly the door in the northern wall opens, revealing the gateway of the north; it is in the form of a low thorn hedge, with a narrow gap in it. Beyond the gap we see a cave within a great wall of rock. Deep within the shadows of the cave we see a faint glow of silver-white light, like starlight.

It our now our intention to travel to the West, to the city of Murias. We turn to look upon the western door, and the vision of a sea lit golden red between two low hills. We pass through the door, and immediately find ourselves in a shallow valley between two low hills. We see the water glowing with a light like sunset, yet we cannot see the sun. A stream runs through the valley, and we follow it towards the sea. As we walk we hear a faint music, the sound of harps playing by sea. The air has a salt taste to it, and we can hear the quiet breaking of waves upon the beach. As we travel through the valley, we see that there are many white stones among the grass, and looking closely realise that these are lumps of quartz. The grass is of a rich green blue colour, tough and springy, and there are spears of wild asparagus growing out of the sandy earth. It seems as if the sea sometimes rises and floods the valley, for the earth is mixed with sand and shells.

As we look at the valley floor, we realise that the stream is flowing towards us: it flows from the sea up into the valley. We pause to meditate on this flowing water, and as we pause we see a fish dart through the water, heading rapidly towards the sea. *(Pause here)*

One by one we bend to drink from the stream: the water is pure and clear, and has no taste of salt. We walk forward, and suddenly emerge at the shore. The sea shines with golden light, but the waves breaking upon the shoreline are rich dark green and blue. We feel the sea, sensing its power and its presence, and pause to affirm our intent to find the hidden city of Murias. *Pause here*. Once again the sound of music rises, as if coming out of the water, and we see two figures appear, one to our right, one to our left. They are tall with long flowing green and white hair: each plays a small richly ornamented harp. Their fingers are long and they have golden nails. As the harpers play we follow the stream towards the sea, passing between the harpers.

Now we approach the water's edge, and as we do so the sea changes, and we can look into it. The shore slopes away into the depths, and we can still see the stream, now widening into a great river, flowing out of the depths of the sea towards us. As if the water has become our natural element, we walk out and it passes over our heads. We breathe water like air, and find that we are following a wide silver river over a rolling countryside. Great streams of green seaweed roll and surge about us, and we feel the currents of the invisible sea.

Far ahead we see the river emerging out of a complex towering set of pinnacles, falling in a silver cloud towards the sandy shore, and gathering to flow up the land. We realise that this is the city of Murias, and pause in silence to focus our attention upon it: the towering pinnacles of glowing white and green rock, the falling silver waterfall. As we look we see shimmering movement in and out of the pinnacles, yet no clear sight of who or what swims there. *(Short pause here)*

We find that as we have contemplated the city, we have floated rapidly towards it: the rock rises directly before us, a translucent white and green complex of spires, pinnacles, caverns, fluted shapes sculpted by water. There is great movement all around us and we hear the faint sound of harps and of voices.

A narrow stair in the green rock leads up to a cave mouth, and from this cave the silver river falls. One by one we climb the narrow steps, and pass through into the cave.

The cavern is filled with a huge bowl of green rock, a vast vessel with silver water bubbling up out of it, pouring over the rim, and flowing away out of the cave mouth. This is the sacred vessel of the west, the city of Murias. As we look upon it a presence hovers over the water, and we look upon the guardian of the cauldron of regeneration. (*Pause here for contemplation. Harp music if possible*)

To each of us a fairy being comes, rising out of the great vessel of stone. They bring us each a small gift, and we in turn, find something that we brought with us and give it to them. These gifts appear suddenly in our hands, and we recognise them, even though we had not realised that we carried them with us. With the exchange of gifts our companions take our hands, and bring us to the edge of the vessel. The rising silver water floods over the lip of the vessel, and for a moment we are touched by the flying drops of spray. As soon as this touch has been received, we are led back to the cavern mouth. There a tiny round boat is moored, tied by a strand of braided weed to a lump of rock. The companions laughingly sign that we must enter this boat, and as soon as we do so, they cast off the mooring. The tiny coracle shoots forwards with great speed and over the edge of the waterfall.

But we do not fall: the boat rises gently over the silver river, and floats towards the high horizon, which we realise is the shore line. We feel many beings swimming with us, laughing, singing, and sometimes they flash for a moment into our vision and out again. Suddenly we rise through the rolling waves, and find that our boat is floating on the surface. It comes to the shore, and we step out by the silver river. Where the green harpers appeared there are two low bushes of grey-green colour. We pass between them and there is a rustle in the gentle wind. We cast long shadows before us, yet when we turn we see the golden path across the waters, but no sun.

Now we pass rapidly up the valley, and the river narrows into a tiny fast flowing stream, flowing impossibly up the slope. We see before us a small dolmen, upright stones with capstones over them. Much of it is covered by sandy earth, but here is a large opening into which the stream flows. We step into this chamber, and find ourselves passing through a door into a square chamber. We return to our outer world, and the chamber dissolves, changing into the familiar place where we began our journey.

Four: The City of Falias in the North

We begin by building strongly in our inner vision the Four Directions of North, East, South, and West. In the North is night and winter; in the East is dawn and spring; in the South is noon and midsummer; in the West is autumn and evening.

As we build our vision of the Directions, we see the room in which we sit change into a square chamber, with a door in the wall of each Quarter, and know that we must pass through each door in turn to reach the four cities of the fairy realm: Gorias in the East, Finias in the South, Murias in the West, and Falias in the North.

EAST: First the door in the eastern wall opens, revealing a familiar landscape beyond. We look upon the gateway of the east: it is in the form of two standing stones, with a narrow gap between them. Through this gap we see a spring landscape, lit by pale blue and green light.

SOUTH: Next the door in the southern wall opens, revealing a familiar landscape beyond. We look upon the gateway of the South: it is in the form of two trees, one of green spreading branches and the other a tree of flame, constantly burning but never consumed. As we look upon these trees, they seem to exchange with one another; first one is flames then of green branches, then the other. We look between them and see a brilliantly lit land, with a distant hill rising directly in the centre of our line of sight.

WEST: Now the door in the western wall opens, revealing a familiar land and seascape beyond. We look upon the gateway of the west: it is in the form of two low hills tinged with the light of evening. Beyond the hills is the sea, with a path of light stretching across it.

NORTH: Lastly the door in the northern wall opens, revealing the gateway of the north; it is in the form of a low thorn hedge, with a narrow gap in it. Beyond the gap we see a cave within a great wall of rock. Deep within the shadows of the cave we see a faint glow of silver-white light, like starlight.

It is our intention to pass through the northern gate, to the city of Falias.

We build the vision of the place beyond the door, and step through the doorway to stand before a low thorn hedge. It is of aged thick thorn bushes, wild and uncut. The branches are black and tangled, and we see only a narrow gap, with branches interlaced over it. Through this gap there is a wall of pale rock, with a narrow cave mouth, like a jagged crack. A faint sliver of light glows and fades from this cave.

As we bend to squeeze through the thorn gap, a sense of presence meets us, and someone steps out from behind the hedge, barring our way with crossed hands, palms outwards. One by one we step up to this warden and state that we have been in Gorias, in Finias, and in Murias, and that now we seek the city of Falias and the sacred stone within it. One by one he lets us enter, but should he turn anyone back, they must await a further journey and seek admission again.

We come through the narrow gap in the hedge, and find that we are in a midnight land. The air is cold and our breath steams: before us is a high wall of pale rock, rising up to a towering cliff far above. We see a band of thick stars in the sky, unlike any sky or constellation that we have ever seen. The gate-warden points to the jagged cave entrance, which now seems totally dark. If we seek the city of Falias and the sacred fairy stone, we must enter this shadowy gate.

Now we step through into the cave, and as we do so we feel hands pull at us and turn us around several times, until we lose our sense of direction. There is no entrance to be seen, and in the dark of the cave we hear soft laughter and the sound of footfalls echoing way into the depths. We pause in the blackness, and realise that it is piled with peace, with stillness, with perfect poise. (*Silent meditation here*)

We affirm that our intent is to travel North, seeking Falias, and even as we do so a faint light appears, which we immediately follow. We feel that the floor of the cavern slopes downwards, yet it is easy to walk, and we have no sense of unease.

Following the faint glowing light, we walk down and down, until we feel the massive presence of the earth, of the aged rock, all around us. Now the way narrows until we have squeezed through, with the smooth rocks touching us on either side. The walls close in until they meet one another, and we stand before a dimly lit niche in which a small clay lamp burns before a round polished stone mirror. The faint reflected glow flickers and fades as the lamp flame moves with the air that we have disturbed. There seems to be no way forward. One by one we look into the small stone mirror, and see reflected there a truth about ourselves. (*Pause for silent contemplation here*)

Having looked within the mirror of the North, we now see the passageway with new vision. The walls leading to the niche have a fine gap, a hairline seam, and we realise that the lamp and mirror are set in a doorway. Even as we realise this, the stone door, with its lamp and tiny mirror, swings silently aside, and we step through into a vast cavern.

We feel a great open space, so immense that we cannot see the far walls or the roof. The floor is of smooth polished stone, with a complex interlaced pattern set into it in faintly glowing white lines like a huge maze, this pattern lead us further into the cavern, and we follow the glowing pattern forward.

Now we see another light source, first faint, then more clearly: it radiates from a cluster of rock growth rising up from the floor of the cavern. They are of white with flashes of crystalline colour, and the centre of this cluster is a tall smooth white stone, resting upon the natural rock outgrowths. As we approach this central place, we hear the sound of stone beating upon stone, in a deep muted resonance, rising up from all about us. A figure takes shape slowly, forming like a cloud over the smooth white stone: as we reach the rocky growths, we look fully upon the face of the guardian of the North, Keeper of the sacred stone. *(Pause for communion here)*

To each of us comes a stone being, who looks deep into our eyes, seeming to read our entire nature. Each stone being holds a fragment or shaped piece of different coloured stone, and we accept these gifts. They sign that we must place them at the foot of the white central stone, and there we see a pile of offerings: tiny coloured stones, fragments of hair, feathers, rings, ancient jewels, dried leaves. As we look the precious objects turn to leaves and feathers, while the feathers and leaves turn to silver and gold. The guardian of the sacred stone laughs at our perceptions, and we feel a deep wisdom and joy in that laugh.

As we look upon the tall white stone, resting in the centre of the rocky crystalline cluster, we see a faint shape within it. It seems to be a sleeping figure, and we look closely at this wonder. *(Silent pause here)*

Now the guardian of the North bids us leave, and the stone beings usher us away, not in the direction by which we came, but to the other side of the sacred place. They march us towards a flight of steps, rising up over a rocky outcrop, lit by tiny glowing lights that seem to burn without flame or smoke, illumination coming directly out of the stone. High above us, we see a gap in the wall of the cavern. We climb the stairs, and as we rise, we see three tiny images far away high in the walls of the cavern. One is a window onto the east, the other is a window onto the south, the third is a window onto the west. We are climbing towards the window of the North.

As we climb we see the sacred stone far below emit waves of white light, and hear again the pulsing sound of stone rubbing on stone, overlaid with flowing tones and resonances. As we reach the top of the stair, we hear a great procession passing by far below, yet see nothing. Our stone-companions have left us, and we stand before a simple wooden shutter. One of us opens this, and it reveals a familiar room with four doors. We pass through, and the wooden shutter closes behind us.

Now our journey to the city of Falias in the North is complete, and we pass out of the fourfold chamber, back into the room where we began our vision. We return slowly to outer consciousness, bringing with us the power of the light within the Earth.

The Fairy Harp

Nor were they long there before they saw draw near them a scolog or 'non-warrior' that wore a fair green mantle having in it a fibula of silver; a shirt of yellow silk next his skin, over and outside that again a tunic of soft satin, and with a timpan (a sort of harp) of the best slung on his back. "Whence comest thou, scolog?" asked the king. "Out of the sidh of the Daghda's son Bodhb Derg, out of Ireland's southern part." "What moved thee out of the south, and who art thou thyself?" "I am Cascorach, son of Cainchinn that is ollave to the Tuatha De danann, and am myself the makings of an ollave (i.e. an aspirant to the grade). What started me was the design to acquire knowledge, and information, and lore for recital, and the Fianna's mighty deeds of valour, from Caeilte son of Ronan." Then he took his timpan and made for them music and minstrelsy, so that he sent them slumbering off to sleep.' And Cascorach's music was pleasing to Patrick, who said of it: 'Good indeed it were, but for a twang of the fairy spell that infests it; barring which nothing could more nearly than it resemble Heaven's harmony.' And that very night which followed the day on which the ollave to the Tuatha De Danann came to them was the Eve of Samain. There was also another of these fairy timpan-players called 'the wondrous elfin man', 'Aillen mac Midhna of the Tuatha De Danann, that out of sidh Finnachaidh to the northward used to come to Tara: the manner of his coming being with a musical timpan in his hand, the which whenever any heard he would at once sleep. Then, all being lulled thus, out of his mouth Aillen would emit a blast of fire. It was on the solemn Samain-Day (November Day) he came in every year, played his timpan, and to the fairy music that he made all hands would fall asleep. With his breath he used to blow up the flame and so, during a three-and-twenty years' spell, yearly burnt up Tara with all her gear.' And it is said that Finn, finally overcoming the magic of Aillen, slew him.

From *The Fairy Faith in Celtic Countries*,
W Y Evans Wentz, 1911

Some powerful traditional motifs are woven into this tale, concerning the living world of Faery, the inhabitants and topography of that realm, the acquisition of magical objects, in this case a Faery Harp, and the aid of faery allies.

The means of descent into the Otherworld, drawn from Gaelic tradition, and made by our unwitting hero in a dream, is still used in visualisations today, and is a classic example of how a traditional image can be employed in both story-telling and active meditation and visualisation. A guided vision using this method of descent is found in Chapter Two.

The mysterious language of Fives makes an appearance here, with some clues as to its encryption and decoding, including a long passage appended to the end of the tale, for those who wish to pursue its meaning further.

Like most dealings with the faery realm and its people, this magical tale is the merest summary of an event that led to a complex set of adventures, and I hope to publish the remainder in due course. The central character is not, of course, myself.

The Fairy Harp

Do you have a flair, a talent for finding things? I do...or rather, I used to. For years I would wake up and know which junk shop, market, sale, to attend. I suppose that I still have that flair now, but have not used it for some time, being occupied with other matters. My house is crammed with prints, carvings, and thousands of books...mostly found through following a blind intuition. Of course, most of it is rubbish, and only of interest to me, though some of the books and prints have values that increase with absurd speed.

Yes, it is an interesting talent; but there is an old adage, hoary wisdom, that we always pay a price for such gifts. This becomes even more bitter when the mild gift gives a greater gift; then the price is heavy indeed. But I run ahead of myself here, a bad habit which I am unable to avoid. So I shall return to the time and place wherein my gift found me a gift, and though the first price, the monetary one, seemed small, the true price was, and is, high.

On a hot sweating day, a Saturday in midsummer, I knew that I had to go to the local antique market...which is a euphemism for junk and bric-a-brac sale. Something, my talent told me, waited there for me. An eighteenth century history book, perhaps, useless to anyone but an obscure author such as myself, a curious walking stick, or, more rare in these avaricious collecto-rified times, an old musical instrument. I have a music room replete with bagpipes, mandolines, Syrian ouds, hammered dulcimers, shawms, old flutes, concertinas, fretless banjos and frail Victorian guitars that never seem to have been played, still redolent of delicate ladies and their musical fashions.

All bought for modest sums, and now valuable to collectors or dealers...but as I am a musician, and was a musician for years before becoming an author, I have no intention of speculating, unless, as sometimes becomes necessary, it be to raise money to buy another instrument.

So I strolled around the market, waiting for my hands to twitch. Oh yes, when I come close to the object which my talent has located from afar, my hands twitch slightly. Parapsychic greed, perhaps.

One stall in particular seemed promising, as it had several large cardboard boxes of books unsorted and unpriced by the dealer... all the best bargains come this way. Once I found a printed translation of the medieval *History of Glastonbury* by William of Malmesbury. Not very interesting in itself, as there are several editions of this famous book, which describes, among other wonders, the (falsified) finding of King Arthur's tomb by the monks of the Abbey. But this happened to be the personal copy belonging, once, to Frederick Bligh Bond, the archaeologist who excavated Glastonbury Abbey in the early twentieth century, according to some very unorthodox theories.

Though proven correct in his archaeological work, and vindicated by the actual finds that he had predicted accurately, Bligh Bond was so publicly ridiculed for his esoteric leanings that he eventually left Britain for America. But somehow his little book remained behind, finding its way by devious routes into my hands. He had made copious pencil notes in every margin, giving insights into many aspects of his own work, and into the lives of other mystics of the period, including Fiona Macleod (the poetic pseudonym of William Sharp), and J.Giles, who translated many of the ancient chronicles from Latin into English in the late nineteenth century. This annotated book also described certain meetings, and the founding of a spiritual order...but that is another story.

So I dug into the boxes of books, hoping to find something of comparable interest at a price low enough to encourage purchase. The dealer was a rather loutish character, smelling of beer even at ten in the morning, unshaven, and sniffing liquidly. I liked him immediately. But after twenty or thirty books on subjects such as Water Board Reports for 1933 in the County of Hampshire, weighty verse dramas by self-published poets, fully indexed guides to the transactions of the Metallurgical Society of Great Britain and Ireland (1897–1912), and many dull moralistic novels, I paused.

Looking up, I saw the dealer hurriedly slip his can under the table, as if he was afraid that I might like a beer for myself. This was a delicate moment, for he knew that I was about to ask for something specific, and (assuming it was not beer) that if he could establish my desires, he could certainly fix a higher price than that possible from a casual purchaser:

"Ah..hmm... do you ever have any old musical instruments?" I murmured indifferently while flipping through a copy of Women's Own from 1967 as if it really interested me, and musical instruments were merely an aside or a flippant question to pass away some time between other more important matters. It may have been my imagination, or so I thought at the time, but he seemed to flinch as if he had been slapped in the face. He looked at me for a long time before replying.

"Musician are you?" he finally grunted.

"Yes" I admitted, knowing that this would be better for pricing anything than being a collector or, heaven forbid, a dealer.

"Well, I've got a crate of old stuff in the van. The usual, you know, bought it as a lot in the auction last week. Sheet music, a few books on music, some letters, there's an old mandoline, and a beaten up kind of harp, more of a toy really. You could have the lot for say...a hundred quid." He looked at me sideways, as if to estimate the effect of this opening figure.

"I'd like to take a look" I said casually, my fingers twitching so hard that I crammed my hands into my pockets. Whatever I had come for was in that crate...but if he was asking a hundred pounds, then it meant that he had probably paid fifteen or twenty for the lot, and would not settle for less than sixty.

He was back within a few minutes, staggering under a large wooden crate, which he slammed, quite deliberately, down onto the concrete floor. Something gave a loud discordant twang from inside.

"Go on then, take look. But I'm not splitting it up, it's all or nothing...hundred quid, round figure. Cost me ninety, so I'm not really making anything, just enough for me petrol to get here today. Take a good look..." And his hand slid cunningly towards the beer can, even as I delved into the crate.

Of course, I found it straight away. The surrounding sheet music, by worthies such as Ethelbert Nevin, seemed to slide away. The broken mandoline fell into one corner, and revealed a small dull brown harp, with a bundle of letters tied with green silk ribbon to the forepillar. It was plain, almost ugly, made with only fifteen strings. But as I touched it, it seemed to tremble, to shift slightly into my hands. This was what I had come for.

But there was a problem...the price. Now if it had merely been a chance found instrument or set of books, I could have haggled with the dealer, but when something is found by flair, by talent, you have to pay the actual price asked or leave it be. A hundred was too much, and I had to somehow find out the real price without conflict, otherwise I was in breach of talent, and might lose my minor psychic skill forever. Remember, no gift without a price.

"I like the harp" I said, clutching it tightly and emerging from the crate. This time he openly took a long pull on his beer, and sat back with a look of clear satisfaction on his face.

"Of course, " I continued hurriedly, "It's only a homemade thing, perhaps an amateur kit or hobby instrument…it would need a lot of work. What about selling me the harp on its own? "

"Sorry matey, can't be done. You buy the sheet music and the mandoline, and I'll give you the harp, but I want to be shot of the lot. Hundred quid. Tell you what, ninety five for cash no receipt."

I waited, desperate to take the harp home, desperate to open that package of letters and see what they contained. But I waited.

"Tell you what… I saw you looking through the books there, take a look at these, perhaps we can make a deal on the lot." And with this he pulled a cardboard box out from beneath the table, right next to his now depleted six-pack of beer. And like a conjuror, he placed two large blue books upon the table-top. My fingers twitched again, but only slightly. They were copies of William Phelps, History of Somerset published in the 19th century.

"I'll throw these in as well, can't get rid of them…there are some nice prints in them though, you could make a bob or two framing them to sell…ninety quid for the lot, and the harp is free." He stressed the gift of the harp, as if it was important, and then, in a rush of frank confession said,

"To tell you the truth, that's how I got it. Somebody's deceased estate…they was to give the harp away to whoever would take it…but the executors put it in to sell with a load of other stuff, conditional, like."

I watched my hands count out nine new ten pound notes. I sold the mandoline and the sheet music to a dealer further down the market, for fifteen pounds, cash no receipt. And with the small harp under one arm, the *History of Somerset* under the other, and the bundle of faded letters in my now hollow cash-depleted pocket, I walked out into the stifling heat of the city in midsummer.

On arriving home, I gave the books only the briefest of attention; they were a complete history of Somerset in considerable detail, from prehistoric times to the nineteenth century, and contained much of interest to the historian, antiquarian, or archaeologist. They were certainly a bargain at whatever proportion of the ninety pounds they had cost. I suddenly realised that these books alone might be worth fifty or sixty or more to a collector, and I had already made fifteen back by selling the bundle of sheet music (also collectible) and the broken mandoline. And the harp…well, he had stressed that the harp came free, and insisted on shaking hands upon it all. As I left he was opening his last beer and smiling.

So, at last, I sat in the quiet of my music room, and untied the green silk ribbon that held the bundle of letters against the forepillar of the harp. I set them carefully down, and turned to look first at the instrument. All fifteen strings were intact, and curiously, they were made of brass, copper, or some similar wire, blackened with age, but still gleaming in places. I rubbed at this patina, and the strings reappeared as bright golden wires of varying gauges, the bass strings being braided and wound to gain thickness and timbre.

The fifteen tuning pins in the harmonic curve were also black, but with a little hard rubbing with a cloth, appeared to, my considerable surprise, to be silver. This dull brown instrument had hidden material qualities. The wood appeared to be oak for the forepillar, and sycamore for the curve. The sound box was carved out of one piece, in the very ancient manner of true Celtic harps, and was of a dark black wood of uncertain type. The sound board was dark brown, with a few stains as if of rusty water, and seemed to be pine or spruce. All good quality materials, plain, undecorated, old.

Finally I ran my hand along the fifteen strings. They produced a mellow but discordant sound, and I reached for my tuning keys. None of them fitted the small silver pins. So I turned to the faded envelopes, and in the first, wrapped in a thick soft fabric like woven grass, there was a bronze tuning key, very ornately wrought with convoluted twists, spirals and shapes. It fitted the silver tuning pins perfectly, and I spent some time setting the strings into a two octave scale. If you know stringed instruments well, you can physically feel the pitch and manner in which they are accustomed to be tuned, the wood settles happily to its familiar tension and shape. The pitch required was low, the scale somehow indeterminate, with no thought of modern tempering.

The sound of that harp was like a lovely voice from another world, from a distant dream-past. I wondered who could have owned such a sweet instrument, and so opened the letters at last, hoping to find some history of the instrument therein...

That night I had a dream so terrifying that I awoke with a jolt, feeling that I had slammed back into my bed after falling from a height. In the dream I was crawling among the roots of a great tree, thick knotted rough boled roots like branches, yet roots they were, stretching and weaving around me into a wide web of tangles and grasping stems. Yet I was not within the earth, for the roots seemed to grow upwards to the sky above, and a strong gravity pulled me ever towards their centre, their origin, which was below me wherever I turned.

As I struggled, crawling aimlessly, twisting and turning one way then another, seeking a way out of the mazy root grip, rasping my hands, tearing my clothes, I suddenly looked down. Far below me I saw the trunk of a mighty tree seeming to fall away, and then spread out into a wide cone, a mountain, a circle of shivering green and silver branches and leaves. The height was terrifying, and my sweating hands slipped upon the rootbark.

Then I awoke, sweating indeed in my midsummer night bed in the centre of the unsleeping city. Nor could I sleep again until dawn and the cool wind that rises at that time. Whenever I closed my eyes I felt myself falling, falling down a huge smooth brown barked tree trunk, down towards the hard ground far below.

The following evening, the weather being still hot and fine, I brought out my polishing kit for the restoration of varnishes and finishes on wooden instruments. The black body, brown forepillar and stained soundboard of the little harp deserved thorough cleaning. The rusty stains upon the fine grained soundboard could, perhaps, be removed, with a mixture of two parts malt vinegar, two of linseed oil, and three parts methylated spirits. Or so I thought.

The sound box and forepillar cleaned well, and began to glow under my attentions, but the soundboard, though much dirt came from it, retained its complex red watermarks. I began to wonder if they were within the wood rather than upon it. In certain lights the stain looked like two faces, in others like a map of two adjoining zones, linked by a thin line.

I tuned the harp several times, and found that it stayed well in tune once it had settled. The wire strings were gleaming now, and seemed to be an alloy of brass, though they shone like gold. I knew that some very early instruments had indeed been strung with gold wires, but considered this highly unlikely for such a plain and functional harp, surely dating from no earlier than the last century.

With this thought in mind I turned again to the letters.

'*I would have you take especial care of the harp*' the first one had read the previous day '*for it is of great value to its owner, and he or she will never be without a co-walker. Yours in both...*' and then one of those stylised complex signatures that was illegible to all except those who knew the writer. No address or date, but the writing was bold and heavily looped, one of the formal hands used in the eighteenth or nineteenth century at a guess. So the instrument was that old. The letter was not addressed to anyone either, no Dear So and So, no Beloved. I recognised the phrase co-walker from somewhere, but could not place it, and yours in both... was obviously an abbreviation of some phrase known to the reader, but its expansion escaped me. There were three further letters, in the same hand. All were surprising, strange, tantalisingly cryptic.

The Second Letter

'A harper wandered by the sea shore, and there he found the body of a beautiful girl, drowned and rotted in the salt waters. He cut off her golden hair and braided it up into harp strings: he took her fine finger bones to make harp seating pins; and her body he floated out into the mother deep to rest.

When he came to a great hall that night, he fitted his dark wooden harp with the golden hair strings, and the fine white bone pins to seat them into the sounding board. The harp struck up of its own accord, and sang:

Woe unto my sister
Woe unto my sister
Woe unto my sister

And a lovely dark haired brown eyed girl in the court screamed aloud and ran headlong from the hall. But the lord and lady of that place set the great ban-dogs after her, for she had murdered her own sister out of spite and jealousy and all for love of a mortal man. The dogs tore her to pieces. The next morning the harper flung his harp into the great river, and it was washed away, floating upon the waters for many days and nights.

And in a hollow of a deep pool made by an old mill dam, long overgrown with willows, the harp came to rest. And there it was found.'

I took this curious opening to be the beginning of a story or perhaps a florid novel by the original owner of the little harp, a fantasy based upon his or her instrument. It reminded me of an old ballad, of a children's dance-game. Though sceptically telling myself that I was a fool, I could not resist looking at the mounting pins on the harp, those used to seat the strings firmly in their holes through the soundboard. They were of, I think, ivory. But the strings were certainly wire and not hair.

That night I was in the tree again. No sooner had I fallen asleep than I found myself trapped and crawling, fumbling through the roots. The only way accessible seemed to be downwards, where they grew thicker and wider, merging into the trunk. I was always forced to travel that way, with my head downwards, though I wanted to turn and climb up, up, to ordinary sky above... the sky that meant my home, the sky over my house in the waking world.

My knees were stuck under my chin, my arms pinned by two great dark roots. I heaved my body through the narrow space between them, and found that I had again moved downwards towards the trunk. I twisted my head around and saw that I was not alone.

Sitting upon a wide major root to my left was a dead girl: her eyes had long been nibbled away by fishes, her flesh was puffed and white, her head bald of hair. Yet she turned towards me, and pointing one fingerless hand downwards, and the other upwards, opened her mouth, revealing green teeth.

"*Ymo gany wit er un daws*" she said in a sweet clear voice. I knew exactly what this meant, though it was no language I had ever heard before. It meant that I would only be free if I climbed down the trunk of the great tree. Then to my great relief, I awoke.

The Third Letter

'*No harpist should be without a consoling song or verse. I commend this rhyme to you, wherever you may find yourself. Yours in both....*

> *IN FIVES I RUN AGAINST THE SUN*
> *MY SPIRIT LOST, TWO CHILDREN GONE.*
> *MY TONGUE DIRECT IS NOW ENCHAINED,*
> *FIVE CROSSED THE BRIDGE*

YET STILL REMAINED.'

This short message, quite incomprehensible, was accompanied by a detailed illustration, finely drawn in ink. It showed a fertile landscape, with a river flowing through it. Lying by the river bank was a large naked woman, of the proportions preferred by Reubens. She seemed to be asleep. A horde of children scampered to and fro over a bridge, while a wild capering man with bald head, seamed wrinkled face and ragged beard, led them over the river. He clutched a collection of fine chains attached, as it seemed, to their tongues. He danced backwards over the bridge towards the far bank, drawing some of the children with him, while others ran in the opposite direction. Five rather forlorn looking infants stood by the sleeping woman, fingering their chainless tongues.

After reading this curious missive, and studying the picture, I refrained for some time from opening the fourth and last letter, hardly daring to guess what nonsense it might contain. And it was only then, when I finally opened that fourth envelope of rich creamy paper, that I realised that they had all been sealed: they were not the keepsakes, the love letters that I had assumed them to be, but were unopened communications...no one had read them before they had come into my possession.

I tried once again to clean the stains from the soundboard of the harp, but the more I cleaned, the more dirt came from the native wood, leaving the red marks intact. I tried looking at them in a mirror, holding the instrument up to catch the light; they reminded me more than ever of a map, of the sort drawn before the introduction of modern contours, with shaded hills and valleys, tracts of forest, mysterious blank areas. I had seen as much, I reminded myself, upon my bedroom ceiling as a child.

That night I began to climb down the tree trunk, shaking with fear, almost paralysed with vertigo. It plummeted away below me, finally opening out into a vast cone of branches and glittering leaves, trembling in the distant wind below. As I emerged from the roots, clambering around onto the base of the trunk, I found that there were deep folds in the bark, and that these made precarious toeholds. As is the way with dreams, I began to climb down the trunk face first, as if I had no common sense to turn round and climb normally.

I emerged from out of the shade of the roots into bright light, of a clarity and quality that I had never experienced before. I could see every detail in the tree bark, every tiny swirl and hue of colour from dark black through brown to subtle reds and pinks, with occasional flushes of rich green. I could see every fold and pattern of the skin of my hands, and the fine hairs normally invisible upon them. So clear was my vision in that light that I began to laugh for sheer pleasure, realising how grey and clouded it had been before. As I laughed, I climbed boldly down, and the wind hit me.

I had seen the leaves shimmering far below, but had not realised the strength of wind necessary to shake them: it laid hold of me and began to push me around the tree trunk to my left, whipping my clothes, tearing at my hair. My eyes filled with tears, and even my mouth was pulled sideways, and my nails began to break and bleed where I gripped hard upon the tree trunk.

Suddenly I was determined that, come what may, vertigo, gales, sea-dead maidens uttering gibberish, I would climb down that tree into the branches below, and on to the ground beyond that. Even as I made this resolution, I could see that a wide land spread out far below, and the wind whipped my head around until I saw a low rounded hill far across the grassy plain.

Then I awoke, to a strange humming wailing sound that rose and fell without rhythm. I staggered from my bed and felt the night wind blowing through the open window, bringing with it the first rain for weeks. It blew against the strings of the little harp where I had set it by my bedside, and this eerie resonance had surely influenced my dream. In future, I said to myself, picking up the harp, this stays where it belongs, in the music room.

But somehow I knew that it did not belong to the music room, irrational though the notion was. It belonged...I took the harp into the kitchen with me, and made coffee. Where did it belong, if not in a music room?

The fourth letter had been useless to me, to say the least.

The Fourth Letter began as follows:

Oc tiu mixa gaas igja ya ypisjiye yma fada ac Cixon taa wijj buas cpah paudisb ymin jiyyip...' And proceeded accordingly for a further short page of neat stylish handwriting. If you wish to read the rest, and struggle with its meaning as I did, I have appended it to the end of this preliminary account of my adventures. Suffice it to say I could not read the message for some time, and by the time I could read it, I knew most of what was in it from hard experience. It ended, as with the previous letters, with the words *Yours in Both* and the florid illegible signature, which I later discovered to simply be the words *A Friend*.

But I was into my third almost sleepless night, and by the fourth day I was exhausted. My work was suffering, and I found myself falling asleep, or rather jolting awake, when I should have been proof-reading. The rain was short lived, and the heat wave reasserted itself. I ran deep cold baths, did press-ups, jogged around the block, much to the amusement of my neighbours who knew that I was an effete arty type. I waited for night.

Late in the evening, the sun shines horizontally into the western windows of my house, tunnelled and reflected from the tall pale sandstone walls of the surrounding buildings, giving a red tinged level light that is unusual, distinctive. It was in that light that I slept, and found myself half-way down the great tree.

In my previous dreams, in the middle of the night, it had been bright noon in the tree place, but now it was early dawn. A pure blue-green light swept up over the land below, so fast that the shadows seemed to run before it. Looking down I saw dim shapes running to keep within the receding shadows, but when I looked again they had vanished, and I thought that I had been mistaken.

As the dawn light increased, I wandered among the branches, and found them at last to widen out, becoming a safe stairway to the ground below. I jumped the last few feet, not onto the hard painful earth of my fears, but onto rich springy turf speckled with tiny white flowers. I immediately looked not around me, but backwards up the tree. It hung above my head for a moment, then my senses inverted, and I felt as if I was floating above it, looking towards its roots, which vanished into a dark muddy swirling hole. Disorientated, I blinked, and when I opened my eyes again, the tree had vanished.

I stood alone, upon a windswept grassy plain that extended to the horizon in all directions. All but one, that is, for far away to the presumed East, where the light had welled up, was the grassy mound that I had first seen when the high winds had tugged me around the tree trunk. There was nowhere else to go.

The ground was helpful, which is to say it bounced slightly under me, and seemed to push me along. The clear light, the fresh air, the rich grass and tiny flowers, combined to invigorate me, until I felt stronger, fitter, cleaner, than I had ever been in my entire sordid dreary life. I broke into a run, and with my eyes fixed upon the distant hill, ran and ran and ran, until I fell panting onto the ground, which yielded to me like a lover, and cradled me like a mother while I sobbed for breath.

Turning onto my back, I discovered that there was no sun to be seen in the sky, but a huge array of impossibly large stars, flickering and glinting with many colours. Some were moving with visible speed, and as I looked several bright lights sped across the sky in different directions, leaving coloured trails.

As I lay there stargazing, an increasing feeling of urgency came upon me. I felt as if someone was reminding me, nudging me, whispering that I should make haste towards the hill. I looked around, but saw no one, yet the sense of presence remained until I started to walk again, after which it faded. So I was on my way again, pleased to find that the grassy hill was closer now. I walked briskly towards it, determined not to lose my breath or over-exert myself again.

I approached the hill at what seemed to be mid-day. As there was no sun in the sky, it was difficult to judge, but the light seemed to clarify and intensify hourly, and if I had arrived at dawn, I reckoned my arrival at the hill to be around noon.

It was larger than I had expected, a rounded grassy mound. Though it had looked small from a distance, it now loomed over me, and I realised that its rounded contour had disguised its true size. It was a huge work; I say work deliberately, for it was artificial, a vast mound raised up long ago, now worn smooth by wind and rain, and grown over with grass.

I decided to climb to the top, but felt a curious warning, a voiceless whisper similar to that which had urged me to hurry towards the mound. I looked round, and saw nothing but grass and flowers waving in the wind. No animals, no tall plants, no trees. I looked again for the giant tree by which I had descended, and thought that I saw, in the direction from which I had come, a shimmering column of air, water vapour, or rainbow light. When I looked hard, the shimmering vanished.

Not knowing what to do, I began to pace around the mound, and as I walked I heard faint sounds like whispers, footfalls, or stifled cries. I could see nothing, that is, I saw nothing until, rounding one end of the mound where it narrowed almost to a point, I came upon a stone box.

This box was a small chamber, like a gate-house, of stone slabs jutting out of the narrow end of the hill. The wind plucked at my sleeve, and seemed to say *'Now go in there'*. I spun around quickly, but saw no one. The stone box was sealed with a large square of dark green granite. I pushed upon this crude door and it tilted back, perfectly hinged and balanced. To my shock a man was sitting hunched inside.

I said a man, but really he was not human. His body was thin and tall, and his head was uncomfortably bent in that narrow space. He wore silver and white armour of the most exotic and outlandish kind, covered in spirals and curves and embossed shapes, with exaggerated pointed shoulders terminating in cascading grey plumes. The armour extended only as far as a kilt or tunic might, for his legs were bare, as were his feet. His skin was of a pale white colour tinged with faintest rose pink and green mottling. He looked up, and I saw his high cheekbones, slanting violet coloured eyes, and hair of deep blue with pure silver streaks. He looked at me slowly, with utter indifference, then quickened his gaze towards something behind me, and scurried out of the box to allow me entrance. When I stood immobile, he leant within and produced a short spiral-headed javelin, made of bone or ivory, and gave me a sharp push with its butt.

I fell into the stone box, and the lid swung shut behind me, leaving me in the dark. I heard a muted sound, rather like a polite and formal cough, the type of noise made by a butler or a very discreet head waiter. Then the inner door swung slowly open, admitting a flood of ruby light, and my first glimpse of the chamber beyond. *'Go on you fool'*, whispered a voice *'Or they'll shut it again'*. So I scuttled through into that red light, and as I entered it transformed suddenly to a vivid gold and green.

The first things that I saw in that place were tall torches fastened, so I thought, to the stone walls. They burned with a brilliant green and gold flame: I looked at the torch nearest to me, and found that it was a root, jutting out of the narrow earthen space between two vast slabs of dark green rock. It blazed with green fire, yet was not consumed, and gave off no smoke. Yet there had been no trees above. I took three steps forward, emerging from under a low lintel of stone, and realised how cavernous that chamber was. It stretched away to my right and left, as if I had emerged from the middle of one side, though I was sure the entrance had been at the narrowest end of the mound.

There were no magnificent furnishings or heaps of treasure, but a huge bare space, the walls lined with enormous stones fitted tightly together, their unbroken surface showing earth only where the root torches appeared. The brilliant green and golden light illuminated every part of the spacious chamber, and cast no shadows. Looking upwards I saw the stone walls taper

143

inward to form the roof, until they met together in a perfect dry seam that ran the full length of that place. The floor of the hall was of polished black slabs, inlaid with fine silver lines in a chaotic disturbing pattern, if pattern it could be rightfully called.

To my left stood rank upon rank of tall warriors with bone white spiral-headed spears in their long fingered hands, and green metal leaf-bladed swords thrust through their belts. They wore a bewildering variety of strange costumes and head gear; feathered plumes, crests of fishes spines, animal heads of gold and silver, crystal caps with delicately carven wings, and tall conical bronze helmets inlaid with green, blue and red enamel and rough unfacetted gems. Some wore armour like that of the gatekeeper, while others sported quilted jackets and short trews heavily embroidered with abstract designs in subtle colours.

A few wore only reptilian scaled leather loin cloths and revealed their tall muscular bodies, their arms and legs wrapped around with heavy massive ornaments in the shape of golden serpents. A small group of these warriors also wore gold serpents coiled around their necks, and these few stood apart from the mass, as if superior or in command, their eyes closed in trance, their arms crossed, their legs evenly spaced apart.

To my right I saw a long table, with immense stone supports and a surface of flat highly polished crystalline rock. Behind this sat a gathering of strangely beautiful men and women in a confusing variety of exotic clothing. Among the many coloured cloaks, embroidered robes, vivid leather kilts, embossed jackets, concealing and revealing hoods, flimsy tunics, some wore nothing but their tattoos upon navel and breasts, while others simply hung jewels, chains, strings of shells and feathers over delicately pastel hued iridescent skin. Though both the men and women, or perhaps I should say males and females, for they were not human, had long flowing heads of hair, none had any hair upon their bodies or faces.

In the centre of this group were two tall thrones. One was roughly cut from a huge rock shot through with translucent crystal, seeming to grow long crystalline spurs and clustered outcrops from every jutting corner, while its crevices held flashes and veins of varicoloured minerals and metals. The second throne was nothing more nor less than a huge hollowed tree stump, out of which living branches sprouted silver and green leaves. I hesitated to approach this great table, and when I looked upon those who sat within the prodigious thrones, began to shake with emotion. I felt filled with awe, with fear, and yet with profound relief, joy, ecstasy.

"Stop all that drivelling, and get on up there before they change their minds" hissed a hard voice in my ear, and I was given a painful blow on the back which made me stagger toward the high table. I looked up into the eyes of

the king of that place where he sat upon and within his rock: he alone of the males there grew a beard. Both his beard and hair were long and curling, a rich dark brown colour with golden strands shining out as if gold had been braided into hair and beard, or as if he had stout golden hairs growing within them. His skin was smooth and swarthy, the golden brown colour and texture of the ripe autumn hazelnut shell. His mouth was firm yet smiling slightly, and his dark black eyes looked upon me, not with the contempt that I had expected, but with amusement.

He wore a simple purple tunic and a long cloak of grey feathers; his arms and feet were bare, like those of most of the people in that place. In one hand he held a huge iridescent cup, made of glowing multi-colored shell, set with silver handles. In the other he held a tiny branch, made of pure white silver, with a golden acorn upon its tip. His nails, I saw, were a dark green, almost black, while the hairs upon his hands and arms were white, and seemed to move and ripple constantly.

Next to this king, for king he surely was though he wore no crown, sat the most exotic and disturbing female that I have ever seen. Her face haunts me even now, and in that wondrous place she outshone all the other beautiful and strange beings like the full moon outshines a candle flame.

Her skin was very pale, and seemed to change colour in slow mobile waves, first a gentle flush of palest green, then a blushing rose pink, a subtle almost invisible violet, then the blue of a wild bird's egg. These colours were so delicate, so subliminal, that it took me some time to realise that they were passing across or through her flesh.

Her hair was very long indeed, reaching over her shoulders and flowing down on either side of her waist, across the rough-hewn arms of the tree trunk throne with its vibrant leafy shoots, and onto the floor. It was of a dark golden red colour, shot through with black streaks, and like a huge cloak it fell about her. Her nose was long and narrow and her mouth wide, her lips of a curious purple colour. As the delicate hues of her skin changed, so did the shade of lips, growing paler, then darker, sometimes to red, sometimes black, sometimes blue.

But her eyes were the most remarkable of all. I say remarkable, for no superlative word could describe or evoke them. I looked upon her eyes, for it was impossible to look into them, and was enthralled. They were a tawny golden colour, like those of a hawk, and the pupils were a void bottomless black. About the hollows of her eye sockets she had silver tattoos, or patterns within her skin. These spiralled in opposite directions leading off in a delicate tracery across her high cheekbones and down either side of her face.

My eyes must have followed the convoluted pattern of these designs as I rudely gazed upon her, for she suddenly smiled, and the silver line on one side of her exquisite jaw widened and became defined as an image of a serpent. Her teeth, when she smiled, were pure white and perfectly formed, each one being pierced with a tiny clear glowing jewel.

From her smiling mouth, my gaze dropped, not unwillingly, but certainly in fear, to her body. Her robe was of a leaf green colour, shot through with many white ribs and veins. Indeed, it might have been a single huge leaf wrapped tightly about her waist and thighs. Her breasts were bare, and there I saw again the serpentine patterns glowing deeply within her shining skin. There was no shame or lewdity to look upon her perfect body, only joy and terror.

I felt the pressure of her gaze upon the top of my head, and slowly looked up again. This time her eyes caught mine, and I was pinned, fixed like a rabbit before the bird of prey. A melodious voice slid through my mind like a razor-sharp ice-cold blood-warm life-devouring blade:

"How short you are. The stature of mortal men has lessened greatly. I doubt if we can use your services here, but perhaps you can take a token back to your people to remind them of us." And with this she held up a small blue flower, a forget-me-not. It seemed to grow out of the outstretched palm of her hand, appearing from within the skin, and then emerging, complete with roots, to slide into her long pale fingers.

I approached the table, and leant over, head bowed, with my hand outstretched. She in turn leaned toward me, and I smelled a perfume of the sap of growing green plants, of rich warm earth, of honeysuckle, mingled with the cold pure scent of deep spring water. Tears came unwilling to my eyes, and I took the tiny plant, wrapping my hand carefully about it. She took great care not to touch my flesh, and I wondered how I might smell to her.

With a tiny movement of her fingers she signed me away from the table, and I stepped blindly back, not caring if I should fall, both regretful and relieved that I need not stand close to her again.

The king then leaned forward and spoke aloud. His voice was the merest thin whisper, yet it ran clearly through that vast hall, and every being in that place raised their heads to listen. Their murmuring, which had been as the sea, fell silent. The eyes of the entranced commanding warriors snapped open and glittered like green ice.

"Go back now, little man. I give you safe conduct, and I see besides that you have a trusted ally who attends you. Leave by the same route by which you entered, and do not stray from the path, whatever you might hear or see."

And with these words, a group of distant musicians struck up a thin eerie sound upon pipes and flutes, while many of the warriors raised wide shallow drums and beat upon them with bones inlaid with wide red stripes. The

sound was deep and complex, high and shocking; the interaction between the drums made the floor and walls tremble, while the wailing pipes caused my hair to bristle and my teeth to ache. The company raised tall glasses, bronze and gold goblets, crystalline cups, wooden bowls, and began to drink healths to one another. Suddenly I was ignored, and I stood gaping about me. In that moment of transition, I realised that there were no harps to be heard or seen.

"Move you slug, before one of the warriors remembers what you are and chooses to hunt you for sport...move!" And a pair of invisible cold rough hands grabbed my arm and dragged me away from the royal table.

I reached the low lintel of stone through which I had entered, and clambered up three steps into the stone box. As I climbed through, the green light seemed to turn a deep cherry red behind me, but when I turned to look back, the stone valve slammed shut with a deep boom, cutting off all light and sound from within. The last sight I had of those beings was the beginning of a wild dance. Then moist air flooded through the outer stone-door as it opened before me, and I stepped out into an evening light, with a cool wind and shadows seeming to approach from my left. The tall warrior in his exotic silver armour leaned nonchalantly against the stones, picking his nails with a long, slim black dagger. He eyed me with hostility, and ceasing his manicure, reached for the spiral-headed short javelin thrust into his plaited gold-wire belt. But he paused, stepped back, and looked behind me. I turned also, yet could see nothing. As I passed him, thinking at every moment that he might attack, he made the slightest of bows, as if to someone who walked beside me. He ducked back into the gate chamber, and pulled the stone down after him. He seemed to be shaking his head in disbelief or disgust.

I knew for certain now that I had an invisible guide or ally; he or she had spoken to me several times, had pushed me forward toward the royal table, had been mentioned by the king within the mound. Finally my ally had grabbed me by the hands, with a cold and rough sensation, as if of scales or perhaps fine chain metal gloves. But I could still see no one, and somehow felt that he, she, or it, had withdrawn now that I was back upon the plain at evening. Gently I put the flower, still fresh in my hand, into my shirt-pocket.

The welling shadows approached in pools and streaks, moving swiftly like patches and clouds of fog passing low over the grass. These were outriders, heralds of a high dark wave of seething blackness far to my left. Whereas the region had been empty when I arrived that morning, it was now full of life. Creatures of all sizes scurried quietly away from the streaks of shadow, from the wall of night. They leapt into burrows that I had missed in full daylight, they gathered in groups and ran swiftly away towards a distant forest line, which I was sure had not been visible when I ran so joyfully in the light towards the great mound. I saw rabbits, deer, wild cats, cattle, foxes, many birds in flocks, and other indistinct shapes that stayed out of vision, skirting round me where I stood. The movement of so many creatures had a lulling hypnotic effect upon me, and I drifted into a stillness, a lethargy, waiting for the darkness to envelop me at last.

One solitary figure approached me and paused just beyond arms length. To my befuddled sight it looked similar to a man, but a man hurriedly designed or made up from poor memory. It shimmered slightly, and I realised that I was looking upon a glamour, an illusion. The sight of it brought me back to my senses, and I began to walk slowly away from it, keeping it in my vision all the while.

"You had best move quickly, mortal man. The Land turns towards the Dark Star, the secret Sun. It is midday in your home place when the Dark Star shines here; a time of terror and doubt. Move quickly, for your ally has departed to go before you and you are alone."

"What are you?" I asked hurriedly, for I had thought at first that this apparition might be my phantom ally.

"I am a sending from the king within the mound, who reminds you not to leave the path. Go now for the terror time approaches."

Even as the shimmering false-man spoke, it fell apart in shreds, and was blown away by the night wind. I realised that I stood upon a tiny faintly glowing slot or deertrack through the grass, and began to move quickly along it, knowing that it would lead me to the great tree.

As I walked, the grass seemed to visibly grow thicker, longer, and pools and coils of shadow slid about within it. I heard distinct high pitched laughter follow me, and footfalls stamping and rustling, and several times the sound of what could only have been huge creatures mating. The light grew purple and then grey and dim, and the towering wall of shadow seemed very close as I reached the tree.

A single branch-tip touched the surface of the ground, as if the entire inverted tree was anchored by a leaf, and the vast cone of branches vanished into deep indigo obscurity above my head. I prepared to climb.

As I touched the branches, two creatures appeared from out of the shadows, seeming to come from within the tree. They were grey and green, covered with moss and creepers, and each had no face, only a wide flat leaf. They touched me gently with their long tendrils, and infused me with a sense of deep peace, the timeless time of growing plants, and perfection of rooting in the earth and reaching slowly but inevitably towards the light. For the first time I understood what it was like to be a tree, a plant, a flower, and I longed to stay with them. Even as I longed, I felt my feet dig into the earth.

In sudden fear I leapt into the branches, and began to climb as fast as I could in the growing darkness, pulling myself up by the feel of the branches, not caring if I cut my hands or lashed my face.

I awoke in the middle of a hot afternoon, lying naked upon the floor of my kitchen, with the harp beside me. I staggered to the shower, and sluiced the sticky sweat from my body. Dressing quickly I scrabbled for the fourth letter, determined this time to break its cryptic language. Within the envelope, tucked into one corner, was a dried flower.

An Interview with the poet A E Russell

In this chapter we have some descriptions of faery beings from the poet and mystic AE, George William Russell (1867–1935). Russell was an artist as well as a writer, and an associate of W B Yeats and his circle of 'Celtic Twilight' and Golden Dawn members. I do not, however, think that his descriptions of the faery beings are literary inventions, though clearly his language is more refined than that of the uneducated Irish men and women interviewed by folklorists. Russell's descriptions are typical of many experiences described to me by modern people who have never read his words or even heard of him.

We begin with his interview with the young Evans Wentz(3), who kept this matter anonymous, as Russell is quoted but not named. Next we have an extract from the autobiography *Candle of Vision*(21) which is recommended reading.

Q.— Are all visions which you have had of the same character?

A.— 'I have always made a distinction between pictures seen in the memory of nature and visions of actual beings now existing in the inner world. We can make the same distinction in our world: I may close my eyes and see you as a vivid picture in memory, or I may look at you with my physical eyes and see your actual image. In seeing these beings of which I speak, the physical eyes may be open or closed: mystical beings in their own world and nature are never seen with the physical eyes.'

Otherworlds.—

Q.— By the inner world do you mean the Celtic Otherworld?

A.— 'Yes; though there are many Otherworlds. The Tir-na-nog of the ancient Irish, in which the races of the Sidhe exist, may be described as a radiant archetype of this world, though this definition does not at all express its psychic nature. In Tir-na-nog one sees nothing save harmony and beautiful forms. There are other worlds in which we can see horrible shapes.'

Classification of the 'Sidhe'.—

Q.— Do you in any way classify the Sidhe races to which you refer?

A.— 'The beings whom I call the Sidhe, I divide, as I have seen them, into two great classes: those which are shining, and those which are opalescent and seem lit up by a light within themselves. The shining beings appear to be lower in the hierarchies; the opalescent beings are more rarely seen, and appear to hold the positions of great chiefs or princes among the tribes of Dana.'

Conditions of Seership.—

Q.— Under what state or condition and where have you seen such beings?

A.— 'I have seen them most frequently after being away from a city or town for a few days. The whole west coast of Ireland from Donegal to Kerry seems charged with a magical power, and I find it easiest to see while I am there. I have always found it comparatively easy to see visions while at ancient monuments like New Grange and Dowth, because I think such places are naturally charged with psychical forces, and were for that reason made use of long ago as sacred places. I usually find it possible to throw myself into the mood of seeing; but sometimes visions have forced themselves upon me.'

The Shining Beings.—

Q.— Can you describe the shining beings?

A.— 'It is very difficult to give any intelligible description of them. The first time I saw them with great vividness I was lying on a hill-side alone in the west of Ireland, in County Sligo: I had been listening to music in the air, and to what seemed to be the sound of bells, and was trying to understand these aerial clashings in which wind seemed to break upon wind in an ever-changing musical silvery sound. Then the space before me grew luminous, and I began to see one beautiful being after another.'

The Opalescent Beings.—

Q.— Can you describe one of the opalescent beings?

A.— 'The first of these I saw I remember very clearly, and the manner of its appearance: there was at first a dazzle of light, and then I saw that this came from the heart of a tall figure with a body apparently shaped out of half-transparent or opalescent air, and throughout the body ran a radiant, electrical fire, to which the heart seemed the centre. Around the head of this being and through its waving luminous hair, which was blown all about the body like living strands of gold, there appeared flaming wing-like auras. From the being itself light seemed to stream outwards in every direction; and the effect left on me after the vision was one of extraordinary lightness, joyousness, or ecstasy.

'At about this same period of my life I saw many of these great beings, and I thought that I had visions of Aengus, Manannan, Lug, and other famous kings or princes among the Tuatha De Danann; but since then I have seen so many beings of a similar character that I now no longer would attribute to any one of them personal identity with particular beings of legend; though I believe that they correspond in a general way to the Tuatha De Danann or ancient Irish gods.'

Stature of the 'Sidhe'.—

Q.— You speak of the opalescent beings as great beings; what stature do you assign to them, and to the shining beings?

A.— 'The opalescent beings seem to be about fourteen feet in stature, though I do not know why I attribute to them such definite height, since I had nothing to compare them with; but I have always considered them as much taller than our race. The shining beings seem to be about our own stature or just a little taller. Peasants and other Irish seers do not usually speak of the Sidhe as being little, but as being tall: an old schoolmaster in the West of Ireland described them to me from his own visions as tall beautiful people, and he used some Gaelic words, which I took as meaning that they were shining with every colour.'

The worlds of the 'Sidhe'.—

Q.— Do the two orders of Sidhe beings inhabit the same world?

A.— 'The shining beings belong to the mid-world; while the opalescent beings belong to the heaven-world. There are three great worlds which we can see while we are still in the body: the earth-world, mid-world, and heaven-world.'

Nature of the 'Sidhe'.—

Q.— Do you consider the life and state of these Sidhe beings superior to the life and state of men?

A.— 'I could never decide. One can say that they themselves are certainly more beautiful than men are, and that their worlds seem more beautiful than our world.

'Among the shining orders there does not seem to be any individualized life: thus if one of them raises his hands all raise their hands, and if one drinks from a fire-fountain all do; they seem to move and to have their real existence in a being higher than themselves, to which they are a kind of body. Theirs is, I think, a collective life, so unindividualized and so calm that I might have more varied thoughts in five hours than they would have in five years; and yet one feels an extraordinary purity and exaltation about their life. Beauty of form with

154

them has never been broken up by the passions which arise in the developed egotism of human beings. A hive of bees has been described as a single organism with disconnected cells; and some of these tribes of shining beings seem to be little more than one being manifesting itself in many beautiful forms. I speak this with reference to the shining beings only; I think that among the opalescent or Sidhe beings, in the heaven-world, there is an even closer spiritual unity, but also a greater individuality.'

Influence of the 'Sidhe' on Men.—

Q.— Do you consider any of these Sidhe beings inimical to humanity?

A.— 'Certain kinds of the shining beings, whom I call wood beings, have never affected me with any evil influences I could recognize. But the water beings, also of the shining tribes, I always dread, because I felt whenever I came into contact with them a great drowsiness of mind and, I often thought, an actual drawing away of vitality.'

Water Beings Described.—

Q.— Can you describe one of these water beings?

A.— 'In the world under the waters – under a lake in the West of Ireland in this case – I saw a blue and orange coloured king seated on a throne; and there seemed to be some fountain of mystical fire rising from under his throne, and he breathed this fire into himself as though it were his life. As I looked, I saw groups of pale beings, almost grey in colour, coming down one side of the throne by the fire-fountain. They placed their head and lips near the heart of the elemental king, and, then, as they touched him, they shot upwards, plumed and radiant, and passed on the other side, as though they had received a new life from this chief of their world.'

Wood Beings Described.—

Q.— Can you describe one of the wood beings?

A.— 'The wood beings I have seen most often are of a shining silvery colour with a tinge of blue or pale violet, and with dark purple-coloured hair.'

Reproduction and Immortality of the 'Sidhe'.—

Q.— Do you consider the races of the Sidhe able to reproduce their kind; and are they immortal?

A.— 'The higher kinds seem capable of breathing forth beings out of themselves, but I do not understand how they do so. I have seen some of them who contain elemental beings within themselves, and these they could send out and receive back within themselves again.

'The immortality ascribed to them by the ancient Irish is only a relative immortality, their space of life being much greater than ours. In time, however, I believe that they grow old and then pass into new bodies just as men do, but whether by birth or by the growth of a new body, I cannot say, since I have no certain knowledge about this.'

Sex among the 'Sidhe'.—

Q.— Does sexual differentiation seem to prevail among the Sidhe races?

A.— 'I have seen forms both male and female, and forms which did not suggest sex at all.'

'Sidhe' and Human Life.—

Q.— (1) Is it possible, as the ancient Irish thought, that certain of the higher Sidhe beings have entered or could enter our plane of life by submitting to human birth? (2) On the other hand, do you consider it possible for men in trance or at death to enter the Sidhe world?

A.— (1) 'I cannot say.' (2) 'Yes; both in trance and after death. I think any one who thought much of the Sidhe during his life and who saw them frequently and brooded on them would likely go to their world after death.'

Social Organization of the 'Sidhe'.—

Q.— You refer to chieftain-like or prince-like beings, and to a king among water beings; is there therefore definite social organization among the various Sidhe orders and races, and if so, what is its nature?

A.— 'I cannot say about a definite social organization, but whether it is instinctive like that of a hive of bees, or consciously organized like human society, I cannot say.'

Lower 'Sidhe' as Nature Elementals.—

Q.— You speak of the water-being king as an elemental king; do you suggest thereby a resemblance between lower Sidhe orders and what mystics called elementals?

A.— 'The lower orders of the Sidhe are, I think, the nature elementals of the mediaeval mystics.'

Nourishment of the Higher 'Sidhe'.—

Q.— The water beings as you have described them seem to be nourished and kept alive by something akin to electrical fluids; do the higher orders of the Sidhe seem to be similarly nourished?

A.— 'They seemed to me to draw their life out of the Soul of the World.'

Collective Visions of 'Sidhe' Beings.—

Q.— Have you had visions of the various Sidhe beings in company with other persons?

A.— 'I have had such visions on several occasions.'

And this statement has been confirmed to me by three participants in such collective visions, who separately at different times have seen in company with our witness the same vision at the same moment.

From *The Fairy Faith in Celtic Countries*,
W Y Evans Wentz, 1911

And I saw, without being able to explain to myself their relation to that exalted humanity, beings such as the ancient poets described, a divine folk who I think never were human but were those spoken of as the Sidhe. I did not see enough to enable me to speak with any certainty about their life, and I do not know that it would serve any useful purpose to detail visions which remain bewildering to myself. Into the lowest of these two spheres I saw with more frequency, but was able to understand but little of what I saw. I will tell one or two visions out of many. I was drawn to meditate beside a deep pool amid woods. It was a place charged with psychic life, and was regarded with some awe by the people who lived near. As I gazed into the dark waters consciousness seemed to sink beneath them and I found myself in another world. It was more luminous than this, and I found one there who seemed like an elemental king. He was seated on a throne, and I saw that a lustrous air rose up as from a fountain beneath the seat and his breathing of it gave him power. The figure was of a brilliant blue and gold opalescence, and the breast, as with many of the higher beings, was shining, and a golden light seemed to pervade the whole body and to shine through its silvery blueness. The tribe he ruled were smaller than himself, and these I saw descending on the right of the throne, their shining dimmed to a kind of greyness, and each one as it came before the throne bent forward and pressed its lips upon the heart of the king, and in an instant at the touch it became flushed with life and it shot up plumed and radiant, and there was a continuous descent on one side of grey elementals and on the other side a continuous ascent of radiant figures, and I know not what it meant. And at another time I saw one of these lesser beings flying as a messenger out of the heart of one greater, and I saw a return to the heart and the vanishing of the lesser in the greater, and I know not what it meant. And at another time I was astonished, for I saw rising out of deep water seven shining and silvery figures, and three on one side and three on another side and one beneath, they held uplifted hands on the hilt of a gigantic sword of quivering flame, and they waved that mighty sword in air and sank again beneath the waters. And after that seven others rose up and they held a great spear, and it they pointed skywards and sank below; and after that arose two carrying a cauldron, and, when they had vanished, one solitary figure arose and it held in its hands a great and glittering stone; and why these beautiful beings should bring forth the four precious symbols of the Tuatha de Danaan I do not know, for that Mid-world, as Usheen travelling to Tirnanoge saw, is full of strange and beautiful forms appearing and vanishing ever about the mystic adventurer, and there are to be seen many beings such as the bards told of: Beings riding like Lir or Mananan upon winged steeds, or surrounded like Angus Oge with many-coloured birds, and why these images of beauty and mystery should be there

I do not know, but they entered into the imagination of poets in the past and have entered into the imagination of others who are still living. I can only surmise that they were given the names of Mananan, Angus, Dana or Lir because they were mouthpieces of the bodiless deities and perhaps sitting on high thrones represented these at the Druidic mysteries, and when the mortal came to be made immortal they spoke to him each out of their peculiar wisdom. In myself as in others I know they awakened ecstasy. To one who lay on the mound which is called the Brugh on the Boyne a form like that the bards speak of Angus appeared, and it cried: "Can you not see me? Can you not hear me? I come from the Land of Immortal Youth." And I, though I could not be certain of speech, found the wild words flying up to my brain interpreting my own vision of the god, and it seemed to be crying to me: "Oh, see our sun is dawning for us, ever dawning, with ever youthful and triumphant voices. Your sun is but a smoky shadow: ours the ruddy and eternal glow. Your fire is far away, but ours within our hearts is ever living and through wood and wave is ever dawning on adoring eyes. My birds from purple fiery plumage shed the light of lights. Their kisses wake the love that never dies and leads through death to me. My love shall be in thine when love is sacrifice." I do not believe that either to myself or my friend were such words spoken, but the whole being is lifted up in vision and overmastered, and the words that came flying upward in consciousness perhaps represent our sudden harmony with a life which is beyond ourselves, we in our words interpreting the life of the spirit. Some interpret the spirit with sadness and some with joy, but in this country I think it will always cry out its wild and wondrous story of immortal youth and will lead its votaries to a heaven where they will be drunken with beauty. What is all this? Poetry or fantasy? It has visited thousands in all ages and lands, and from such visions have come all that is most beautiful in poetry or art. These forms inhabited Shelley's luminous cloudland, and they were the models in the Pheidian heart, and they will be with us until we grow into their beauty and learn from them how to fulfil human destiny, accomplishing our labour which is to make this world into the likeness of the Kingdom of Light.

From *The Candle of Vision* by A E (George William Russell)

As I was walking all alane,
   Between a water and a wa'
   'twas there I spied a wee wee man
   He was the least I ever saw.

His legs were but a scthathmont's length
   But thick and thimber was his thighe,
   Between his brows there was a span,
   Between his shoulders there was three...

He took up a muckle stane,
   And flung it far as I could see,
   Though I had been a michty wight,
   I couldna liften it to my knee!

From the Scottish ballad: *The Wee Wee Man*

The Three
Conditions of Being
and Consciousness

Yeats, William Butler (1865–1930). He is chiefly remembered as a great poet, but he is also central to the renaissance of Irish folklore at the end of the 19th century, the close associate of Douglas Hyde, Lady Wilde and Lady Gregory. His *Irish Fairy and Folk Tales* (1888) is a standard work, and *The Celtic Twilight* (1883) made Irish traditions fashionable in England. He was himself a firm believer in FAIRIES, and he dabbled in various forms of spiritualism, but he also took part in practical matters, was an ardent nationalist and a promoter of the arts. And in spite of his mysticism and of the wistful music of his fairy poems -

> Come away! O human child!
> To the woods and waters wild,
> With a fairy hand in hand,
> For the world's more full of weeping than you can understand.

– in spite of these, Yeats is fully aware of the earthy and matter-of-fact quality of fairy tradition in the country.

From *A Dictionary of Fairies* by K Briggs

Communicated Teachings from the Underworld

The word *conditions* refers to states of consciousness, but also refers to conditions of being, to states of existence. No firm distinction is made between the two in the Faery and Underworld tradition, where locations or realms (dimensions) are created by the interaction between the consciousness/energy of the land, zone, and planet (power of place) and that of its inhabitants (power of people).

By inhabitants we mean all beings within the land and within its Underworld dimensions, all the living creatures, human, and other orders of life, that people a location. Some locations, such as sacred sites and anonymous power places, expand into many realms in the Underworld; other locations will have a less complex inner pattern. Whatever the relative complexity of a place or its people, the Three Conditions described in the received teaching which follows may be experienced.

Voices

There are voices within voices. We partake of a spoken tradition with no books. The first voice, if you are able to hear it, is the simple and powerful source. There are others which elaborate and elucidate, and it is possible to listen to one voice or another, and to ask for elucidation if you wish. The listener and seer may also rework the words, but there are some tales, verses, phrases, and powerful words that should not be changed. If you change them, even if you try earnestly to clarify them, they lose power.

All of our teaching and tradition may be received, arising as simple words and visions from the depths, with other voices adding to the stream as it rises. The source teachings are heard by the listener as distinct voices with recognisable tones, and all additions cover these voices or mask their tones, even though they develop their stories.

Such received words come to you from three conditions (see figure 6). Most voices heard in the silence come from the third condition known as the Voice of Many, and even this condition is closed to people living only on the surface. When the ear is opened first there is a great babble and roar as of a crowd or a battle. In this roar some voices are heard immediately and distinctly, while others are faint and confused. This sea of many voices may be heard briefly as you fall asleep, but is lost when you cross the threshold in either direction. It may also be heard as an intrusive muttering by some when they first enter the silence, but if this muttering is pursued, it slips away.

There are those who ardently seek to pursue the Voice of Many, and desire to have contact with the speakers and mutterers. This is like snatching words from a multitude, or thrusting through a great throng and inviting them to

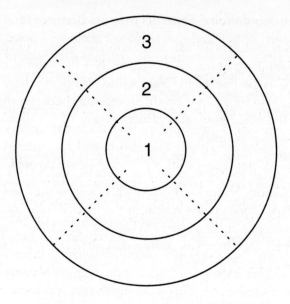

1 = The Voice of One: core voices and inspiration

2 = Voice of Few: specific teachers of tradition

3 = Voice of Many

4 = Yourself, embodying al three

Figure 6   The Three Conditions

come to you. Those at the edge will jostle to reach you at the centre, while those at the centre and closest to you will hasten to the edge in the press of the crowd pushing inwards.

The third condition is like a sea of echoes from the voices that you have heard since childhood, but it is not limited to your memory alone, for it holds an ocean of memories. As a child learns to shut the ear to all voices and sounds but those that have meaning in life, and to respond only to sounds within certain zones of distance, so must you. The zones of close, intermediate, and distant, are reversed in importance in the Underworld. There the furthest and deepest voice is the most precious, and the nearest may be ignored.

The second condition holds the voices of teachers. They communicate a steady flow of clear tuition, either as instructions for your work or as tales and verses. They will also issue images and glimpses of places with the words, for those that see. One listener may hear several teachers or only one, but usually a small number, well defined. The experienced seer and listener can distinguish between voices and can attune to them by choice and at will, rather than by chance. This condition is known as the Voice of Few. These are sometimes heard as clear quiet voices that speak close to your ear, though faery beings are also heard in this way.

The first condition is like the voice of the Land or, if you are strong, the World. It speaks through deep places and appears to the seer as certain of the older gods and goddesses. The first condition will also utter directly, with prophetic power. When this prophetic power flows through a particular place, it also speaks directly through the prophets and poets of that place, as with Merlin and Taliesin. This is called the Voice of the One.

In ancient temples the priestess would remain within the sacred enclosure of earth or water and wait for the voice to utter through her. The oracular priests and prophets, however, were wanderers, often driven wild by the Voice of the One. This indicates a truth concerning the Mystery of Man and Woman and the Sacred Land. This is the truth that was to be turned aside by the story of Adam and Eve.

The direct voice is frequently confused in the mind with the Voice of Many. People who hear for the first time assume that they are hearing a deep spirit or an elevated spirit, when they are only hearing babble. The Voice of the One is rare, and talks in potent riddles, in words heard by the body and the soul more than the mind. When it comes to the prophet or sybil the whole body utters it with voice, tears, and movement.

This whole utterance should never be confused with possession by spirits: the Voice of the One casts all talkative spirits away, and can even destroy them if they are insistent. When the Voice of One is heard the Voice of Many falls silent, and you are set free of it.

Ancestors

Question: How do the three conditions relate to ancestral communication, ancestral memory, ancestral wisdom?

Ancestral voices may be heard in any of the three conditions, but they are often heard foremost within the Voice of Many. The Summoning of the Ancestors is not just the opening of ears to the third condition and the Voice of Many, for you may hear that without any ancestral summoning, even though there will always be some ancestral voices present. The Summoning causes all voices heard to be ancestral, and others to fade away, washed aside in the ancestral tide.

The Summoning also gives access to the deep supply of ancestral memories, which are as if they are your own memories and not through voices alone. Ancestral memory comes through the range of recovered senses, of sight, sound, smell, and touch, and is just as you might touch, smell, hear and see and remember the sensations. It also comes through the range of recovered thoughts and feelings, just as if they are your own feelings. It all comes at once as in a sudden flood.

After this flood of recovered experiences, you will hear their voices. You must wait calmly for the flood to ebb, and remain like a rock. This is why in holy places you hold to your ancestral stone and wrap your arms around it.

When you hear Ancestors speaking with the Voice of Many they will cry out for revenge against past wrongs. You must resist this demand however just it is. Yet you may and should feel both anger and sorrow at the wrongs revealed to you. Within the urge for revenge find compassion; feel the sorrows of your people, learn from their suffering, transform it within yourself, for you are their future. This sea of memory can become unbearable, a terrible tide through the soul. Here is where ancestors speaking from the second condition will help, for the voices of the few are wise.

Ancestors in the second condition will reveal how the sorrows and trials have led to slow changes, how the secret currents of life and the land flow through you and your people over many ages, through generations. One generation or more will cry out for revenge, but beyond their own time they cannot extend unless they are awake in the second condition.

Ancestors speaking with the Voice of Few will reveal the true powers of your people and their holy places, which are not always those assumed and taught on the surface. Voices of the wise do not talk of destiny, race, or obligation, but only of families of unfathomed extent and their stones and springs.

Those speaking with the Voice of Few will lead you to other ancestral lines hidden within your main line, and enable you to open the way to those memories also. They will also bring you to the threshold where you shall hear ancestors speaking within the Voice of One, or reveal to you ways by which you shall come to it unaided.

When ancestors speak within the first condition, the Voice of One, they are the Land. These are the First Ones embodied within the Land, and they are, or become, the prime parents of any and all who live within the land for a number of generations. This number is seven for absorbing into the third condition of the Land, in which all voices (Ancestors speaking with the Voice of Many) are of that land. Before seven generations the Voice of Many will speak from several lands according to your ancestry.

Some come to the First Ones immediately, some only after seven or more generations have passed and the prime parents may perceive them. Thus it is possible by seeking the First Ones as true parents to pass directly from the third to the first condition. This is one of the Mysteries of imprisonment and liberation that you must enter and pass through within the Underworld.

When you move within the second condition you may have access at will to ancestral lines, either of the Land of your generations, or of other lands that they once inhabited. Whereas the first condition voices will be of the Land or of other lands according to your generations, and you may have little will over it, the second condition voices are always of the Land unless you will otherwise.

Some people have several prime parents in the first condition, making a balanced pattern like petals around a flower. Some have less, forming the shapes of triangle, square, or pair only, depending upon their land, their people, and their moving about the world. Each prime parental shape has special abilities that emerge upon the surface: the most flexible and powerful shapes for this present age are those of many or of a pair. In previous ages the potency has been in three and fourfold parentage where lands in the same zone have caused their peoples to move and intermingle. Today the prime parents of any one land and the multiple parentage of many hold the keys to the first condition for the entire world.

Prime Parents And Other Worlds

The prime parents of any one land or of many lands lead the way to the Original Man and Woman, but the prime parents of three or four lands intermingled may close this way. The Original Man and Woman are not of this world at all, so deep contact with ancestors in the first condition leads through the Earth to other worlds. This is one of the Mysteries of acceptance that you shall find within the Underworld, but you are not able to follow its path until you have truly accepted your own Land and world.

Ancestral Memory And Reincarnation

Memory of previous lives and ancestral memories are not identical. Ancestral memories are communicated through the blood, but other lives need not be of the current bloodline. Other lives hold patterns that surface in the present life, but ancestral memories do not always hold such patterns. While ancestral memories are of the body, other lives are of the starry nature that utters many bodies, often with varying bloodlines.

With practice you will distinguish between the memories of the blood and the memories of the star of lives. *Extract from teachings*.

The Princess Of Colchester (*Traditional tale*)

Long before Arthur and the Knights of the Round Table, there reigned in the eastern part of England a king who kept his Court at Colchester. He was witty, strong, and valiant, by which means he subdued his enemies abroad, and planted peace among his subjects at home. Nevertheless, in the midst of all his glory, his queen died, leaving behind her an only daughter, about fifteen years of age. This lady, from her courtly carriage, beauty, and affability, was the wonder of all that knew her. But as covetousness is the root of all evil, so it happened here. The king, hearing of a lady who had likewise an only daughter, for the sake of her riches, had a mind to marry her, and though she was old, ugly, hook-nosed, and hump-backed, yet all this could not deter him from doing so. Her daughter was a yellow dowdy, full of envy and ill-nature; and, in short, was much of the same mould as her mother. This signified nothing, for in a few weeks the king, attended by the nobility and gentry, brought his deformed bride to his palace, where the marriage rites were performed. They had not been long in the court before they set the king against his own beautiful daughter, which was done by false reports and accusations. The young princess, having lost her father's love, grew weary of the court, and one day, meeting with her father in the garden, she desired him, with tears in her eyes, to give her a small subsistence, and she would go and seek her fortune; to which the king consented, and ordered her mother-in-law to make up a small sum according to her discretion. She went to the queen, who gave her a canvas bag of brown bread and hard cheese, with a bottle of beer; though this was but a very pitiful dowry for a king's daughter. She took it, returned thanks, and proceeded on her journey, passing through groves, woods, and valleys, till at length she saw an old man sitting on a stone at the mouth of a cave, who said, "Good morrow, fair maiden, whither away so fast?" "Aged father," says she, "I am going to seek my fortune." "What hast thou in thy bag and bottle?" "In my bag I have got bread and cheese, and in my bottle good small beer. Will you please to partake of either?" "Yes," said he, "with all my heart." With that the lady pulled out her provisions, and bade him eat and welcome. He did so, and gave her many thanks, saying thus: "There is a thick thorny hedge before you, which will appear impassable, but take this wand in your hand, strike three times, and say, 'Pray, hedge, let me come through,' and it

will open immediately; then, a little further, you will find a well; sit down on the brink of it, and there will come up three golden heads, which will speak; and whatever they require, that do." Promising she would, she took her leave of him. Coming to the hedge, and pursuing the old man's directions, it divided, and gave her a passage; then, coming to the well, she had no sooner sat down than a golden head came up singing-

> "Wash me, and comb me,
> And lay me down softly."

"Yes," said she, and putting forth her hand, with a silver comb performed the office, placing it upon a primrose bank. Then came up a second and a third head, saying the same as the former, which she complied with, and then pulling out her provisions, ate her dinner. Then said the heads one to another, "What shall we do for this lady who hath used us so kindly?" The first said, "I will cause such addition to her beauty as shall charm the most powerful prince in the world." The second said, "I will endow her with such perfume, both in body and breath, as shall far exceed the sweetest flowers." The third said, "My gift shall be none of the least, for, as she is a king's daughter, I'll make her so fortunate that she shall become queen to the greatest prince that reigns." This done, at their request she let them down into the well again, and so proceeded on her journey. She had not travelled long before she saw a king hunting in the park with his nobles. She would have shunned him, but the king, having caught a sight of her, approached, and what with her beauty and perfumed breath, was so powerfully smitten that he was not able to subdue his passion, but proceeded at once to courtship, and after some embraces gained her love, and, bringing her to his palace, caused her to be clothed in the most magnificent manner.

This being ended, and the king finding that she was the King of Colchester's daughter, ordered some chariots to be got ready, that he might pay the king a visit. The chariot in which the king and queen rode was adorned with rich ornamental gems of gold. The king, her father, was at first astonished that his daughter had been so fortunate as she was, till the young king made him sensible of all that happened. Great was the joy at court amongst all, with the exception of the queen and her club-footed daughter, who were ready to burst with malice, and envied her happiness; and the greater was their madness because she was now above them all. Great rejoicings, with feasting and dancing, continued many days. Then at length, with the dowry her father gave her, they returned home.

The hump-backed sister-in-law, perceiving that her sister was so happy in seeking her fortune, would needs do the same; so, disclosing her mind to her mother, all preparations were made, and she was furnished not only with rich apparel, but sugar, almonds, and sweetmeats, in great quantities, and a large bottle of Malaga sack. Thus provided, she went the same road as her sister; and coming near the cave, the old man said, "Young woman, whither so fast?" "What is that to you?" said she. "Then," said he, "what have you in your bag and bottle?" She answered, "Good things, which you shall not be troubled with." "Won't you give me some?" said he. "No, not a bit, nor a drop, unless it would choke you." The old man frowned, saying, "Evil fortune attend thee!" Going on, she came to the hedge, through which she espied a gap, and thought to pass through it; but, going in, the hedge closed, and the thorns ran into her flesh, so that it was with great difficulty that she got out. Being now in a bloody condition, she searched for water to wash herself, and, looking round, she saw the well. She sat down on the brink of it, and one of the heads came up, saying, "Wash me, comb me, and lay me down softly," as before, but she banged it with her bottle, saying, "Take this for your washing." So the second and third heads came up, and met with no better treatment than the first; whereupon the heads consulted among themselves what evils to plague her with for such usage. The first said, "Let her be struck with leprosy in her face." The second, "Let an additional stink be added to her breath." The third bestowed on her for a husband but a poor country cobbler. This done, she goes on till she came to a town, and it being market-day, the people looked at her, and, seeing such a mangy face, all fled but a poor country cobbler, who not long before had mended the shoes of an old hermit, who, having no money, gave him a box of ointment for the cure of the leprosy, and a bottle of spirits for a stinking breath. Now the cobbler, having a mind to do an act of charity, was induced to go up to her and ask her who she was.

"I am," said she, "the King of Colchester's daughter-in-law." "Well," said the cobbler, "if I restore you to your natural complexion, and make a sound cure both in face and breath, will you in reward take me for a husband?" "Yes, friend," replied she; "with all my heart!" With this the cobbler applied the remedies, and they worked the effect in a few weeks; after which they were married, and so set forward for the Court at Colchester. When the queen understood she had married nothing but a poor cobbler, she fell into distraction, and hanged herself in wrath.

The death of the queen pleased the king, who was glad to be rid of her so soon, and he gave the cobbler a hundred pounds to quit the Court with his lady, and take her to a remote part of the kingdom, where he lived many years mending shoes, his wife spinning thread.

From *The History of the Four Kings of Canterbury, Colchester, Cornwall, and Cumberland, their Queens and Daughters*. Chap-book, Falkirk, 1823.

One Eye, Two Eyes,
Three Eyes

Mr W B Yeats has given this explanation:- 'Many poets, and all mystic and occult writers, in all ages and countries, have declared that behind the visible are chains on chains of conscious beings, who are not of heaven but of the earth, who have no inherent form, but change according to their whim, or the mind that sees them. You cannot lift your hand without influencing and being influenced by hordes. The visible world is merely their skin. In dreams we go amongst them, and play with them, and combat with them. They are, perhaps, human souls in the crucible – these creatures of whim.' And bringing this into relation with ordinary fairies, he says:- 'Do not think the fairies are always little. Everything is capricious about them, even their size. They seem to take what size or shape pleases them.' In The Celtic Twilight Mr Yeats makes the statement that the 'fairies in Ireland are sometimes as big as we are, sometimes bigger, and sometimes, as I have been told, about three feet high.'

Mrs X, a cultured Irishwoman now living in County Dublin, who as a percipient fulfils all the exacting requirements which psychologists and pathologists would demand, tells me that very frequently she has had visions of fairy beings in Ireland, and her own classification and description of these fairy beings, chiefly according to their stature, are as follows:- 'Among the usually invisible races which I have seen in Ireland, I distinguish five classes. (1) There are the Gnomes, who are earth-spirits, and who seem to be a sorrowful race. I once saw some of them distinctly on the side of Ben Bulbin. They had rather round heads and dark thick-set bodies, and in stature were about two and one-half feet. (2) The Leprechauns are different, being full of mischief, though they, too, are small. I followed a leprechaun from the town of Wicklow out to the Carraig Sidhe, 'Rock of the Fairies', a distance of half a mile or more, where he disappeared. He had a very merry face, and beckoned to me with his finger. (3) A third class are the Little People, who, unlike the Gnomes and Leprechauns, are quite good-looking; and they are very small. (4) The Good People are tall beautiful beings, as tall as ourselves, to judge by those I saw at the rath in Rosses Point. They direct the magnetic currents of the earth. (5) The Gods are really the Tuatha De Danann, and they are much taller than our race. There may be many other classes of invisible beings which I do not know.' (Recorded on October 16, 1910)

From *The Fairy Faith in Celtic Countries*,
W Y Evans Wentz, 1911

What the Big Man taught

The Big Man taught me many things, but the best of them is the story of the Fall, which was never a fall but rather a loving embrace.

"In the beginning", he said, "the world was in many places. Yet it longed to be in one place at one time and yearning drew in its presence into a few places only. In the heart of the stars great ones of light and power felt the world draw in, just like a breath inhaled and held tight. One of the star beings saw her and loved her then, knowing that she must exhale and that she could not, and that her fullness would destroy her in time. So he fell from the furthest star, through the Sun and through the planet Venus, into the Earth, who was still holding her breath.

Now as the Bright One came into the Earth, many lesser beings were drawn in also like burning flames in his wake, a cloak of light weaving through the stars, and perhaps it was her, daughter of the Great Mother, who drew them all in with her holy breath, for the Mother was of her and in her also, She who draws all things unto herself. And when the saints took up the story, handed down in poems, dreams, and visions of the first breath of the World, they called this bright one Lucifer, who is the light of Venus in the morning and evening. And they said he was a fallen archangel, out of Heaven. And they said that when he fell many angels fell with him, so many in fact, that God and Jesus had to shut the heavenly gates, for fear that they might have no hosts to shout holy holy holy any more. And those that fell into the Earth were the faery races, sons and daughters of Lucifer, star-cousin to the Sun, reflected to us in Venus. And this reflection of Lucifer through Venus is one of the great Mysteries of Liberty.

And now the Earth is breathing out. She has been doing so since before the coming of mankind, for Lucifer burning within her causes her to exhale and come into being in many worlds. First she breathed out the smallest of living creatures, so small that they cannot be seen, only their effects can be felt. Then she breathed out the first plants and grasses. Then she breathed out the fishes and the land animals. And all the while the faery races were in and on the Earth, excelling in beauty and light.

Then the Sun spoke to the Earth also, responding to her changing breath, which was like the utterance of a sound or word as she exhaled. And the first men and women, partaking of the nature of above and below, sons and daughters of the Earth and Sun appeared, still soft spongeous and mutable, on the surface of the Earth. Immediately her Breath blew through them, so that for long ages they absorbed her exhalations and were composed of many animals and fishes. But they also absorbed the angelic sounds, the powers of the Sun, Moon, and Planets, which defined them, and gave them yearning beyond their mutability.

So the men and women yearned for the stars beyond the earth, moulded as they were by the sounds of the angels. And they longed for the Earth, moulded as they were by her divine breath that caused all creatures that ever were and ever will be to be moulded into them. So they became divided within themselves, and through that pride that comes from excess longing, turned away from the wisdom of the Lordly Ones, the faery races, and behaved only as if they were animals. For the words and sounds of the angels were to come into perfection through the faery union with humans, the angels of above and below balanced through men and women, who in themselves held all the living creatures. But when mankind abandoned the faery wisdom, they became imbalanced, for they heard only the word of the Sun, and not that of the stars within the Earth.

So the Sun consulted with other Stars, and a great Being was sent into the World, to unite Lucifer, the faery races, the animals, and the humans. And the Great One was to achieve this unity through the humans, who were still capable of joining with the faery races and the living creatures, to make a whole being that was the final pure breathing out of the world. And this Great One travelled right into the centre of the world, through the Sun, the Planets, and the Moon, linking all together. And in the heart of the world he harmonised with Lucifer, to bring great changes to the world, which are still surfacing today."

Extract from an early 18th century journal

In this classic fairy tale we find the theme of Threes again, this time as three sisters. The tale contains many typical rationalised elements among its primal magical themes. I would recommend that you use this story to build a vision, not according to its obvious narrative, but according to the images. This iconographic approach has been discussed by Robert Graves in his *Greek Myths* and *The White goddess*, and it certainly applies to folk ballads and tales.

Take each image, such as the three sisters with their distinct appearances and eyes, the goat, the tree, and so forth, rather than the passages of the tale that seek to explain them. The sisters were once a triple goddess, the goat is her sacred animal, and the tree is the World Tree. The images are the foundation of the tale, not the words. Good luck and never eat fairy apples.

One-eye, two-eyes, and three-eyes

There was a woman who had three daughters, of whom the eldest was called One-eye, because she had only one eye, in the middle of her forehead; the next one Two-eyes, because she had two eyes like other people; and the youngest Three-eyes, because she had three eyes, and the third was likewise in her case in the middle of her forehead. But because Two-eyes did not look any different from other human beings, her mother and sisters could not bear her. They said to her, "You, with your two eyes, are no better than the common folk; you do not belong to us." They pushed her about and threw her old clothes, and gave her nothing to eat but the scraps left over, and made her suffer in every way they could.

It happened that Two-eyes had to go out into the field to tend the goat, but was very hungry, because her sisters had given her so little to eat. So she sat down on a ridge and began to weep, and wept so much that two little streams flowed from her eyes. And once when she looked up in her distress, a woman stood by her who asked, "Two-eyes, why do you weep?"

Two-eyes answered, "Why should I not cry? Just because I have two eyes like other people my sisters and my mother cannot bear me, push me about from one corner to another, throw dish clouts at me, and only give me the scraps left over to eat. Today they have given me so little that I am still quite hungry."

The wise lady replied, "Little Two-eyes, dry your face. I will tell you something, and that is you need not feel hungry any more. Just say to your goat:

'Little kid, bleat, bleat,
　　Little table, I would eat.'

and there will appear a freshly-laid table with delicious food on it, of which you may eat as much as you like. And when you are satisfied and do not require the table any longer, just say:

> "Little kid, bleat, my dear,
> Little table, disappear,'

then it will vanish before your eyes." With that the wise woman went away.

Two-eyes thought, "I must try at once and see if what she says is true, for I am so hungry," and said":

> "Little kid, bleat, bleat,
>
> Little table, I would eat."

Hardly had the words been spoken before a table stood there covered with a little white cloth, and on it a plate, with a knife and fork and a silver spoon, and the most delicious eatables spread round, smoking and still hot as though they had just come from the kitchen.

Then Two-eyes said the shortest grace she knew, "The Lord make us truly thankful. Amen," and set to and ate heartily. When she had had enough she repeated what the wise woman had taught her:

> "Little kid, bleat, my dear,
>
> Little table, disappear."

The little table and everything on it at once disappeared. "That is a nice sort of house-keeping," thought Two-eyes, and was quite happy and cheerful.

In the evening when she came home with her goat, she found a little earthen bowl of food that the sisters had placed for her, but she did not touch it. The next day she went out again with her goat and left the few crusts set aside for her. The first and second time the sisters noticed nothing, but when it happened every time, they remarked upon it and said, "Something must be wrong with Two-eyes; she leaves her food untouched every time, yet she used to eat up all that was provided for her; she must have found some by other means." In order to arrive at the truth of the matter One-eye resolved to accompany Two-eyes when she drove the goat out to the pasture, and to keep watch on her movements and see whether any one brought her food and drink.

When Two-eyes was ready to start, One-eye stepped up to her and said, "I will go with you into the field and see that the goat is well tended and brought to a place where there is enough fodder."

But Two-eyes perceived what One-eye meant to do, and drove the goat out into long grass, saying, "Come, One-eye, we will sit down together; I want to sing you something." One-eye sat down, tired from the unaccustomed walk and the heat of the sun, and Two-eyes sang over and over again:

> "One-eye, are you waking?
> One-eye, are you sleeping?"

And then One-eye shut her eye and went to sleep. When Two-eyes saw that One-eye slept soundly and could not discover anything, she said:

> "Little kid, bleat, bleat,
> Little table, I would eat."

and seating herself at her table she ate and drank till she was satisfied. Then she cried again:

> "Little kid, bleat, my dear,
> Little table, disappear."

and everything disappeared immediately.

Two-eyes now awoke One-eye and said, "One-eye, you try to keep watch but fall asleep, while the goat might stray all over the place; come, we will go home."

Then they went home and Two-eyes again left her little dish untouched. One-eye could not inform her mother why she would not eat, and gave as an excuse, "I fell asleep out of doors."

The next day the mother said to Three-eyes, "This time you must go and watch whether Two-eyes eats out of doors, and whether anyone brings her food and drink, for she must eat and drink secretly."

So Three-eyes stepped up to Two-eyes and said, "I will go with you, too, and see whether the goat is well tended and given enough fodder."

But Two-eyes saw her motive and drove the goat out into long grass, and said, "We will sit down over there, Three-eyes; I want to sing you something." Three-eyes sat down, tired with the walk and the heat of the sun, and Two-eyes sang over again the same little song:

> "Three-eyes, are you waking?"

But instead of singing as she ought:

> "Three-eyes, are you sleeping?"

she sang from carelessness:

> "Two-eyes, are you sleeping?"

and continued:

"Three-eyes, are you waking?
Two-eyes, are you sleeping?"

Three-eyes then shut two of her eyes and slept, but the third, to which the little rhyme was not addressed, did not sleep. Three-eyes did indeed shut it, but only out of cunning, as though it, too, was asleep; but it blinked and could see everything quite well. And as Two-eyes imagined Three-eyes to be fast asleep, she said her little verse:

"Little kid, bleat, bleat
Little table, I would eat."

then ate and drank to her heart's content, and afterwards bade the table begone:

"Little kid, bleat, my dear,
Little table, disappear."

But Three-eyes had seen everything.

Two-eyes came up to her and awoke her, saying, "Ah, Three-eyes, have you been asleep? You can watch well! Come, we will go home."

When they got home, Two-eyes again ate nothing, and Three-eyes said to the mother, "I know now why the conceited creature does not eat: when she says to the goat out of doors:

'Little kid, bleat, bleat,
Little table, I would eat.'

a table stands before her covered with delicious food much better than we have, and when she has had enough, she says:

'Little kid, bleat, my dear,
Little table, disappear,'

and everything disappears; I saw it all exactly. She sent two of my eyes to sleep with a little rhyme, but the one in my forehead fortunately kept awake."

Then the envious mother cried, "Do you want to fare better than we do? You shall wish in vain for the future!" She brought a butcher's knife, and stuck it into the goat's heart so that the creature fell dead.

When Two-eyes saw that, she went out full of sorrow, sat down on the ridge in the field and shed bitter tears.

At once the wise woman appeared again beside her and said, "Little Two-eyes, why do you weep?"

"Have I not good reason to cry?" she answered. "The goat that had my little table spread so nicely every day, whenever I repeated your little verse, has been killed by my mother; now I must again suffer hunger and thirst."

The wise woman said, "Two-eyes, I will give you some good advice. Ask your sisters to give you the dead goat's entrails, and bury them in the ground in front of the house door, and it will bring you luck."

With that she disappeared, and Two-eyes went home and said to the sisters, "Dear sisters, give me just something from my goat; I do not ask for anything good, only give me the entrails."

Then they laughed and said, "You may have that, if that is all you want."

Two-eyes took the entrails and buried them in the evening, when all was quiet, in front of the door, according to the wise woman's advice.

The next morning, when they all awoke and went out of the front door, there stood a wonderfully fine tree with leaves of silver and fruit of gold hanging between them, and there could certainly have been nothing more beautiful or costlier in the world. But they did not know how the tree had come there in the night. Only Two-eyes noticed that it had grown out of the remains of the goat, for the tree stood exactly on the spot where she had buried them.

The mother said to One-eye, "Climb up, my child, and take the fruit off the tree for us."

One-eye climbed up, but whenever she tried to take hold of one of the golden apples the branch slipped out of her hand; and this happened every time, so that she could not break off a single apple, try in whatever position she would.

Then the mother said, "Three-eyes, you climb up; you can look round better with your three eyes than One-eye."

One-eye scrambled down and Three-eyes climbed up, but Three-eyes was no more successful, and strive as she might the golden apples swung back.

At last the mother became impatient and climbed up herself, but could take hold of the fruit no better than could One-eye or Three-eyes, and always caught at the empty air.

Two-eyes then said, "I will go up; perhaps I shall fare better."

The sisters called out, "You, with your two eyes; what can you do?"

But Two-eyes climbed up, and the golden apples did not draw back from her; it was just as though they came towards her hands, so that she could pick off one after the other and brought down a whole apron full. The mother took them from her, and instead of treating poor Two-eyes any better, the mother and One-eye and Three-eyes were so jealous that she alone could pick the fruit that her lot was even harder than before.

It happened once that as they were standing together by the tree, a young knight came by.

"Quick, Two-eyes," called the two sisters, "crouch down that we need not be put to shame by you," and hastily they threw over poor Two-eyes an empty barrel that stood by the tree, and thrust the golden apples she had been picking under it as well.

When the knight drew near, he turned out to be a handsome lord. He admired the splendid tree of gold and silver, and said to the sisters, "To whom does this beautiful tree belong? Whoever will give me a branch of it may ask what she likes for it."

One-eye and Three-eyes replied that the tree belonged to them, and they much wanted to break him off a bough. They each tried very hard, but could not do it, for the branches and fruit swung away from them at every effort.

Then said the knight, "It is indeed curious that the tree should belong to you and yet you have not the power to break off anything from it."

They persisted that the tree was their property; but while they were speaking Two-eyes let a couple of golden apples roll out from under the barrel, so that they ran along to the feet of the knight, for Two-eyes was angry at One-eye and Three-eyes for not speaking the truth. When the knight saw the apples he was astonished, and asked where they came from. One-eye and Three-eyes answered that they had another sister, but she did not let herself be seen, because she had only two eyes like any ordinary person. But the knight wanted to see her, and cried, "Two-eyes, come forward."

Thus encouraged, Two-eyes came from under the barrel, and the knight was astonished at her beauty and said, "You, Two-eyes, can doubtless break me off a branch from the tree."

"Yes," replied Two-eyes, "that I can well do, for the tree belongs to me," and, climbing up, she broke off a branch with its silver leaves and golden fruit, and handed it to the knight.

He then said, "Two-eyes, what shall I give you for it?"

"Ah!" answered Two-eyes, "I suffer hunger and thirst, sorrow and want, from early morn till late at night; if you would take me with you and deliver me, I should be happy."

The knight then lifted Two-eyes on to his horse and brought her home to his castle. There he gave her beautiful clothes, food and drink to her heart's content, and, because he was so fond of her, he was betrothed to her, and the wedding was held with great rejoicings.

When Two-eyes had been taken away by the handsome knight, the two sisters greatly envied her good fortune. "Yet we still have the wonderful tree," they thought, "even if we cannot break off any fruit from it, everyone will stop before it and come to us and spread the fame of it; who knows what we may reap!"

But by the next morning the tree had disappeared and their hopes with it; and when Two-eyes looked out of her little room, she saw to her joy that it stood outside and so had followed her there.

Two-eyes lived happily for a long time. Once two poor women came to her at the castle begging for alms. When Two-eyes looked into their faces she recognized her two sisters, One-eye and Three-eyes, who had fallen into such poverty that they were obliged to wander from door to door seeking their bread. However, Two-eyes bade them welcome and treated them well and cared for them, so that they both regretted from their hearts all the unkindness they had done to their sister in their youth.

The Faery Realm and Its Inhabitants in The Secret Commonwealth

THE FAERY REALM AND ITS INHABITANTS IN *THE SECRET COMMONWEALTH*

One of the most useful summaries of faery traditions is the small hand-written book produced by the Reverend Robert Kirk, writing in 1691 or 1692. Kirk was an Episcopalian minister, working with Gaelic speaking people in the midlands of Scotland, in the Aberfoyle region (near Stirling). He was also a seventh son, and likely to have the Second Sight or healing powers himself. Tradition says that he did not die, but passed physically into the faery realm through the hill at Aberfoyle which bears his name to this day. He is still in the faery realm, and will teach those who seek him out.

His book was not published until the 19th century, when Andrew Laing edited an incomplete and rather confused edition in 1893. More recently an academic limited edition was published by the Folklore Society in 1976, edited by Stewart Sanderson. In 1990 I edited and commented upon the Secret Commonwealth (1), bringing much of the text into modern English where necessary for the general reader. This is the only complete modern edition with a full commentary upon the esoteric traditions found in Kirk's text.

We can build a clear picture of Kirk's understanding of the fairy seership, and healing traditions of the Highlanders. In the following list only Kirk's text is used, and no parallels or variants are drawn in from other sources, though these are abundant and found in our other chapters and quotes.

1   There is another world or dimension that mirrors our own: it is located underground or within the land. The cycle of energies and events in that place is a polarised image of our own, thus they have summer when we have winter, day when we have night, and so forth.

2   The inhabitants of this world are real beings in their own right, and have substantial supernatural powers.

3   Certain people, mainly male seers (but this is Kirk's protective attitude, see *p.203*), are gifted with the ability to see such beings from the mirror – or underworld, and to receive communications from them.

4   The subterranean people are able through signs and mimicry or dramatic actions to show seers what will come to pass in the human world. It is up to the seer to develop means of interpretation.

5   Humans can and do transfer physically to the fairy or underworld.

6   The subterranean people are linked to the land, each region having its counterpart in the underworld. Thus they are, in one respect, identical to the genii loci of the ancient world.

7   The spirits of the dead and of ancestors are also found in this underworld, though they are often distinct from the fairy race themselves.

8   Both the subterranean people and the seers who perceive them retain fragments of ancient religious and philosophical tradition, often at variance with the religious and scientific viewpoints of the day.

9   There are, or were in Kirk's day, spiritual or psychic healers in the human world who work through methods laid down by tradition, often using unorthodox prayers and incantations to accompany their healing ceremonies. These are sometimes of a different category to the seers, and do not receive aid exclusively from the subterraneans, ancestors, or underworld beings and fairies. Kirk also describes healing through prayer, innate virtue, and with faery aid.

Extracts From The Secret Commonwealth

(Adapted for this book by the author. Headings in italics and brackets such as (nature of faery beings) are my own, as are words inserted in brackets in the main text to clarify meanings and ideas.)

(Kirk's book begins...)

An Essay of the Nature and actions of the Subterranean and for the most part Invisible people, heretofore going under the names of ELVES FAUNS and FAIRIES or the like among the Low-Country Scots, and termed hubhsisgedh, caiben, lusbarten, and siotbsudh among the Tramontaines (Highlanders) or Scottish-Irish, as they are described by those who have the second sight: and now, to occasion further enquiry, collected and compared.

Of the Subterranean Inhabitants

(Physical and metaphysical nature of faery beings)

These siths or Fairies, which they call sluaghmaith or the good people: it would seem, to prevent the dint of their ill attempts: for the Irish usually bless all they fear harm of, are said to be of a middle nature betwixt man and Angel, as were daemons thought to be of old: (are) of intelligent Studious Spirits, and light changeable bodies, like those called Astral, somewhat of the nature of a condensed cloud, and best seen in twilight. These bodies are so pliable through the subtlety of the spirits that agitate them, that they can make them appear or disappear at pleasure. Some have bodies or vehicles so spongeous thin and dessicate that they are fed only by sucking into some fine spirituous liquor (essence) that appears like pure air or oil. Others feed more grossly upon the core substance of corn and liquor or on corn itself, that grows on the surface of the Earth; which these fairies do steal away, partly invisible, partly preying upon the grain as do Crows and Mice.

Wherefore in this same age (ie in the present time) they are sometimes heard to bake bread, strike hammers, and to do such like services within the little hillocks where they most haunt. (The great age of some faeries)

Some whereof were old before the Gospel dispelled paganism, and in some Barbarous places as yet, enter houses after all are at rest, then set the kitchens in order, cleansing all the vessels. Such drudges go under the name of Brounies (Brownies). When we have plenty, they have scarcity at their homes; and on the contrary, for they are not empowered to catch as much prey as they please everywhere. Their robberies notwithstanding, oftentimes (they) occasion great ricks of corn not to bleed so well, as they call it, or to prove so copious by very far as was expected by the owner.

(Holism of living creatures described)

Their bodies of congealed air are sometimes carried aloft, while others grovel in different shapes, and enter into any cranny or cleft of the Earth where air enters, (as if) to their ordinary dwellings. The Earth being full of cavities and cells, and there being no place or creature but is supposed to have other animals, greater or lesser, living in, or upon it, as inhabitants; and (there is) no such thing as pure wilderness (ie a vacuum void or emptiness of life) in the whole Universe.

(Humans replace faeries on the surface of the land)

We then, of the more terrestrial kind, having now so numerously planted all countries, do labour for that abstruse people, as well as for ourselves. Albeit when several countries were uninhabited by us, they had their easy tillage, above ground as we (do) now, the print of whose furrows do yet remain to be seen on the shoulders of the very high hills, which was done when the champagne (ie prime or virgin arable land) was still wood or forest.

(Faery processions or "rides" on Quarter Days)

They remove to other lodgings at the beginning of each Quarter of the year, so traversing until doomsday, being impatient of staying in one place, and finding some ease by sojourning and changing habitations, their Chameleon-like (ie changeable of colour) bodies swim in the air, near to the Earth with bags and baggage. And at such revolutions of time, Seers or men of the second sight, females being but seldom so qualified, have very terrifying encounters with them, even on highways. Therefore (seers) usually shun to travel abroad as these four seasons of the year, and thereby have made it a custom to this day among the Scottish-Irish (Gaelic speaking Highlanders), to keep Church duly every first Sunday of the Quarter, to sene or hallow themselves, their corn and cattle, from the shots and stealth of these wandering Tribes. And many of these superstitious people will not be seen gain in Church till the next quarter begins, as if no duty were to be learned or done by them, but the only use of worship and sermons were to save them from those (fairy) arrows that fly in the dark.

(Social order among faeries)

They (the Fairies) are distributed in Tribes and orders; and they have children, nurses, marriages, deaths and burials, in appearance even was we (do), unless they so do for a mock-show, or to prognosticate some such things (that will come) to be among us.

(Faeries and Seers at Funerals)

They are clearly seen by those men of the second sight to eat at funerals, banquets; hence many of the Scottish-Irish will not taste meat at those meetings, lest they have communion with, or be poisoned by them. Also they are seen to carry the bier or coffin with the corpse, among the Middle-Earth men (ie mortals) to the grave.

(Seers see faery doubles of humans)

Some men of that exalted Sight, whether by art or nature have told me that they have seen at those meetings a double-man, or the shape of the same man in two places; that is, a Superterranean and a Subterranean Inhabitant perfectly resembling one another in all points, whom he (the seer) could easily distinguish one from another by some secret tokens and operations, and so go (directly to) speak to the (real) man his neighbour, passing by the apparition or resemblance of him.

(Seers teach a holistic worldview)

They (the Seers) avouch that every Element and different state of being, has (in it) Animals resembling those of another Element, (just) as there be fishes sometimes caught at sea, resembling Monks of (a) late order, in all their hoods and dresses. So as (a result of this resemblance) the Roman (Catholic) invention of good and bad daemons and guardian Angels (is) particularly assigned, (and) is called by them (ie the Seers) an ignorant mistake sprung only from this original (resemblance or reflection of species through the Elements).

THE LIVING WORLD OF FAERY

(More on the double or Co-Walker)

They call this Reflex-man a coimimeadh or Co-walker, every way like the man, as a Twin-brother and Companion, haunting him as his shadow and is oft seen and known among men, resembling the Original, both before and after the Original is dead. And (this Co-walker) was also often seen, of old, to enter a house; by which the people knew that the person of that likeness was to visit them within a few days.

(Faery companions or allies come by invitation)

If invited and earnestly required, these companions make themselves known and familiar to men, otherwise, being in a different state and Element, they neither can nor will easily converse with them.

(The "Great Eater": see also the tale of The Six Servants)

They (the Seers) avouch that a Heluo or great-eater has a voracious Elve to be his attender, called (a) geirt coimitheth, a joint-eater, or just-halver, feeding on the pith and quintessence of what the man eats, and that therefore he continues lean like a hawk or a heron, notwithstanding his devouring appetite.

Yet it would seem that they convey that substance elsewhere, for these Subterraneans eat but little in their dwellings, their food being exactly (ie fastidiously) clean, and served up by pleasant children like enchanted puppets.

(Faery dwellings described)

Their houses are called large and fair, and, unless at some odd occasions, unperceivable by vulgar eyes, like Rachland and other Enchanted Islands; having for light continual lamps, and fires, often seen without fuel to sustain them.

Women are yet alive who tell (that) they were taken away when in child-bed to nurse fairy (spelt ffayrie) children, a lingering voracious image of theirs being left in their place, like their reflection in a mirror, which, as if it were some insatiable spirit in an assumed body, made first semblance to devour the meat, that it cunningly carried by, the then left the carcass as it expired, and departed thence, by a natural and common death.

The (fairy) child and fire, with food, and all other necessaries, are set before the Nurse, as soon as she enters, but she neither perceives any passage out, nor sees that these people do in other rooms of the Lodging. When the child is weaned, the nurse either dies, or is conveyed back, or gets to choose to stay there.

(Gaining and losing sight and knowledge of faeries)

But if any Superterranean (ie human) be so subtle as to practice sleights (tricks) for procuring a privacy (ie knowledge of) any of their (Fairy) Mysteries, such as making use of their ointments, which as Gyge's ring, makes them invisible or nimble, or casts them into a trance, or alters their shape, or makes things appear at a vast distance, and so forth, they smite them (the human concerned) without pain as (if) with a puff of wind. And thus (the fairies) bereave them of both their natural and acquired sights in the twinkling of an eye, (for) both those sights, where once they (are) come, are in the same organ and inseparable. Or they (may) strike them dumb.

(Faery clothing and speech)

Their apparel and speech is like that of the people and country under which they live: so they are seen to wear plaids and variegated garments in the Highlands of Scotland and Suanochs (sunach or tartan) heretofore in Ireland. They speak but little, and that by way of whistling, clear, not rough.

Their women are said to spin, very finely, to dye, to tissue and embroider; but whether it be as (a) manual operation of substantial refined stuffs with apt and solid instruments, or only curious cobwebs, impalpable rainbows, and a fantastic imitation of the actions of more terrestrial mortals, since it transcended all the senses of the seer to discern whither, I leave to conjecture, (just) as I found it.

(Spiritual and holistic philosophy of the seers and of the faeries)

Their men travel much abroad (ie far and wide), either presaging or aping the dismal and tragical actions of some amongst us, and have also many disastrous doings so of their own, (such) as Convocations, wounds, and Burials, both in the Earth and air. They live much longer than we (do), yet die at last, or at last vanish from that State (in which they live). For it is one of their Tenets that nothing perishes, but, as the Sun and (the) Year, everything goes (around) in a Circle, Lesser or Greater, and is renewed, and refreshed in it revolutions. As it is another (Tenet) that Every Body in the Creation moves, which (movement) is a sort of life, and that nothing moves but what has another Animal moving on it, and so on, to the utmost minute corpuscle that's capable to be a receptacle of Life.

(How the seers contact faery allies)

The Tabhaisder or Seer that corresponds with this kind of Familiar, can bring them with a spell to appear to himself or (to) others whenever he pleases, as readily as the Endor Witch did those of her own kind... He is not terrified with their sight when he calls them, but seeing them by surprise, as he often does, frightens him extremely. And gladly he would be quit of such (sights), for the hideous spectacles seen among them, (such) as the torturing of some wight, earnest ghastly staring looks, skirmishes, and the like. They do not (do) all the harm which they appear to have power to do; nor are they perceived to be in great pain, save that they are usually silent and sullen.

(Faery books of magic, charms, and metaphysics)

They are said to have many pleasant Toyish Books. But the operation of these pieces (of literature) only appears in some paroxysms of antic Cory-bantic jollity, as if ravished and prompted by a new spirit entering into them at that instant, lighter and merrier than their own. Other Books they have of involved abstruse sense, much like the Rosicrucian style. They have nothing of the Bible, only collected parcels of Charms and counter-Charms; not to defend themselves withal but to operate on other Animals' for they are a people invulnerable by (ie to) our weapons.

(Spiritual status and condition of the faery people)

Some men say their continual sadness is because of their pendulous state, like those men Luc.13.26, as uncertain (as to) what at the last Revolution (of the World) will become of them, when they are locked up into an unchangeable condition. And if they have any frolic fits of mirth, it is as the constrained grinning of a Mort-head (Death's-head), or, rather as (it might be) acted on a stage, and moved by another, (rather) than cordially coming (to laughter) of themselves. But other Men of the second sight being illiterate and unwary in their observations, vary from these (interpretations and comments).

(Doctrine of souls and reincarnation as taught by the seers)

One averring those subterranean people to be departed souls attending a while in their inferior state, and clothed with bodies procured through their Alms-deeds in this Life called cuirp dhaondachbach, which means fluid active, ethereal vehicles to hold them(selves together), that they may not scatter, nor wander and be lost in the Totum (Plenum or Fullness), or (in) their first nothing (the Void.) But if any are so impious as to have given no alms, they say (that) when the souls of such do depart, they sleep in an inactive state until they resume Terrestrial Bodies again.

(Astral phantasms)

Others, those which the Lowland Scot calls a wraith, and Irish eug or death-messenger, appearing sometimes as a little rough dog, and if crossed, and conjured (beneficially) in time will be pacified by the death of any other creature instead of the sick man, are only exuded fumes of the Man approaching death. (These are) exhaled and congealed into a various sickness, as ships and armies are sometimes shaped in the air, and (are) called Astral Bodies, agitated as wild-fire with (the action of the) wind, and are neither Souls nor Counterfeiting Spirits.

(Faeries are not astral bodies, but independent beings)

Yet not a few vouch, as is said, that surely these are a numerous people by themselves, having their own polities (ie systems of society and government). This diversity of judgements may occasion several inconsistencies in this (my present) Rehearsal (of fairy-lore) after the narrowest scrutiny (has been) made about it.

(Faery weapons)

Their weapons are mostly solid earthy bodies, nothing of iron, but much of a Stone similar to yellow soft flint (and) shaped like a Barbed arrow head, but flung as a dart with great force. These arms, cut by art and tools it seems beyond human (skill), have somewhat of the nature of a thunder-bolt, subtly and mortally wounding the vital parts without breaking the skin. Some of these wounds I have observed in beasts, and felt them with my (own) hands. They (ie the Fairies) are not as infallible (as) Benjamites, hitting at (ie to within) a hairs breadth; nor are they wholly unvanquishable, at least in appearance.

(Raptures of the Second Sight)

The men of that second sight do not (simply) discover strange things when asked, but at (ie in) fits and Raptures, as if inspired with some Genius at that instant, which before did lurk in or about them. Thus have I frequently spoken to one of them who in his transport(ed state) told (that) he cut the body of one of these (fairy) people in two with his iron weapon, and so escaped this onset (of the Second Sight). Yet he saw nothing left behind of the apparently divided body. At other times he out-wrestled some of them.

(Seer vanishes and reappears)

His neighbours often perceived this man to disappear at a certain place and then about one hour after to become visible (again) and discover himself (ie reveal himself) nearly a bow-shot from the first place. It was in that place where he became invisible, said he, that those subterraneans did encounter and combat with him.

(Examples of the Second Sight)

A man of the second sight perceived a person standing next to him, (and) sound (of health) to others' view, wholly gored in blood, and he (the Seer), amazed like, bid him instantly flee. The whole (ie healthy) man laughed at his art and his warning, since there was no appearance of danger; he had scarce contracted his lips from laughter, when unexpectedly an enemy leapt in at his side and stabbed him.

(Ceremonies and means of passing on the Second Sight)

There be odd solemnities at (the) investing (of) a man with the privileges of the whole Mystery of this Second Sight. He must runs a tedder of hair, which bound a corpse to a bier, in a helix about his middle from end to end, and then bow his head downward [as did Elijah I Kings,18,42], (and) then bow his head downwards, and look back through his legs until he see a funeral advance, till the people cross two Marches; or (he may) look thus back(wards) through a hole where these a know of fir (in a fir-tree). But if the wind changes point while the hair tedder is tied about him, he is in peril of his life.

The usual method for a curious person to get a transient (ie temporary) sight of this otherwise invisible crew of Subterraneans, if impotently and over-rashly sought, is to put his foot on the Seer's foot, and (then) the Seer's hand is put on the inquirer's head, who is (then) to look over the wizard's (seer's) right shoulder. (This method is one) which has an ill appearance, (for it implies) as if by this ceremony an implicit surrender were made of all between the wizard's foot and his hand before the persons can be admitted (as) a privado to the art (of seership).

Then will he see a multitude of wights like furious hardy men flocking to him hastily from all quarters, as thick as atoms in the air. These are not nonentities or phantasms, (or) creatures proceeding from an affrighted apprehension (or) confused or crazed sense, but realities appearing to a stable man in his wakening senses and (thus) enduring (ie undergoing) a rational trial of their being. These (beings), through fear, strike him breathless and speechless, but the see or wizard, defending the lawfulness of his skill, forbids such horror, and comforts his novice (ie pupil) by telling of Zacharias being struck speechless at seeing of apparitions [Luke 1,20].

Then he further maintains his art by vouching Elisha to have had the same (vision) and (that he) disclosed it thus to his servant in 2 Kings, 6,17 when he blinded the Syrians, and (also) Peter in Acts 5,9, foreseeing the death of Sapphira, by perceiving, as it were, her winding sheet about her before-hand. And (the seer also cites) Paul in Corinthians 12,4, who got such a vision and sight as should not, nor could, be told. Elisha, also, in his chamber, saw

Gehazi his servant at a great distance taking a reward from Naaman, 2 Kings 5,26. Hence were the (biblical) prophets often called Seers, or men of second and more exalted sight than others.

(Training of seers)

Also the seer trains his scholar by telling of the gradations of nature, (which are) ordered by a wise providence; that (just) as the sight of bats and owls transcends that of shrews and moles, so the visive (ie visual) faculties of men are clearer than those of owls, (and just) as (the visive faculties of) eagles, lynxes, and cats are brighter than mens'. And again (the seer teaches) that men of the Second Sight, being designed to give warnings against secret engines (ie devices and occurrences) surpass the ordinary vision of other men, which is a native habit in some, descended from their ancestors, but acquired as an artificial improvement of their natural sight in (the case of) others.

The sight of such seers resembling in their own kind (ie way) the usually artificial helps of optical glasses, (such) as perspectives, telescopes, and microscopes, without which adscititious (ie supplementary) aids, these men here treated of (ie discussed) do perceive things that for their smallness of subtlety and secrecy are invisible to others, though (they may be) daily conversant with them.

(Nature and transmission of the Second Sight)

They (the seers) having such a beam (of light) continually about them, (such) as that of the sun, which when it shines clearly only, lets common eyes see the (dust) atoms in the air, (fragments) that without these rays they could not discern.

Some have this second sight transmitted from father to son through the whole family, without their own consent or the teachings of others, proceeding only from a bounty of providence, it seems, or by a compact, or a complexional quality of the first acquirer (of the sight).

(Healing powers of seventh sons)

As it may likewise seem strange, yet nothing vicious, in the (cases of) such as Mr Greatrakes, the Irish stroker (ie healer), seventh sons, and others that cure the King's-Evils, and chase away diseases and pains, with only (ie nothing more than) stroking of the affected part (of the body).

Which (ability), if it be not the relic of miraculous operations, or some secret virtue on the womb of the parent, which increases until seven sons be born and decreases by the same degrees afterwards, proceeds only from the sanative (ie curative) balsam of their healthy constitutions. Virtue goes out from them by spirituous effluxes into the patient, and their vigourous healthy spirits affecting the sick, (just) as usually the unhealthy fumes of the sick infect the sound or whole (ie healthy).

(Second Sight temporarily proven to a sceptic)
It is usual in all magical arts to have the candidates prepossessed with a belief of their tutors skill and abilities to perform their (magical) feats, and act their juggling pranks and legerdemain. But a person called Stewart possessed with a prejudice against all that was spoken of this second sight, and living near to my house, was so put to it by a seer before many witnesses, that he lost his speech, and the power of his legs, and breathing excessively, as if expiring, because of the many fearful wights appearing unto him; the company were forced to carry him into the house.

Lord Tarbott's Letter To Robert Boyle (as quoted by Kirk)

A succinct account of my Lord of Tarbott's relations in a letter to the Honourable Robert Boyle Esquire, of the predictions made by seer whereof himself as ear and eye-witness. I thought fit to adjoin hereunto, that I might not be thought singular in this disquisition, that the matter of fact might be undeniably made out, and that I might with all submission give some annotations with animadversions on his supposed causes of that phenomenon, with my reasons of dissent from his judgement.

(Tarbott's report on the Second Sight)
Sir,
I heard very much but believed very little of the second sight, yet its being affirmed by several (people) of great veracity I was induced to make enquiry after it in the year of 1652, being then confined to abide in the North of Scotland by the English usurpers. The more general accounts of it were that many Highlanders, (and) yet far more islanders were qualified with this second sight, that men women and children indistinctly were subject to it, and children where parent were not: sometime people came to age (with it) who had it not when young, nor could any tell by what means (it was) produced. It is a trouble to most of them who are subject to it and they would be rid of it at any rate if they could.
The sight is of no long duration, only continuing so long as they can keep their eye steady without twinkling (blinking). The hardy therefore fix their look that they may see longer, but the timorous see only glances, their eyes always twinkling at the first sight of the object.
That which is generally seen by them are the species of living creatures and of animate things which are in motion, such as ships and habits upon persons.

They never see the species of any person who is already dead. What they foresee fails not to exist in the mode and in that place where it appears to them. They cannot well know what space of time shall intervene between the apparition and the real existence. But some of the hardiest and the longest experience have some rules for conjectures, (such) as if they see a man with a shrouding sheet in the apparition, (then) they will conjecture at the nearness or remoteness of his death by the more or less of his body that is covered by it.

(Seeing at a distance)

They will ordinarily see their absent friends though at a great distance, sometimes no less than from America to Scotland sitting standing or walking in the some certain place, and then they conclude with assurance that they will see them so and there. If a man be in love with a woman they will ordinarily see the species (vision or double) of that man standing by her, and so likewise if a woman be in love, and they (the seers) conjecture at their (the lovers) enjoyments of each others by the species touching of the person, or appearing at a distance from her, if they enjoy not one another. If they see the species of any person who is sick to death they see them covered over with the shrouding sheet.

These general (instances) I had verified to me by such of them as did see and were esteemed honest and sober by all the neighbourhood, for I enquired after such for my information. And because there were more of these seers in the Isles of Lewis, Harris, and Uist than in any other place, I did entreat Sir James MacDonald, who is now dead, Sir Normand Macleud, and Mr Daniel Morrison, a very honest parson, who are (all) still alive, to make enquiry into this uncouth sight and to acquaint me therewith, which they did, and all found an agreement in these general (instances), and informed me of many (other) instances, confirming what they said. But though (they are from) men of discretion and honour, being but (reports) at second hand, I will choose rather to put myself than my friends on the hazard of being laughed at for incredible relations (ie stories).

(Seer has vision of death of a landlord)

I was once travelling in the Highlands, and (had) a good number of servants with,me, as is usual there. One of them going a little before me (and) entering into a house where I was to stay all night and going hastily to the door, he suddenly stepped back with a screech, and did fall by a stone which hit his foot. I asked what the matter was, for he seemed to be very much frightened. He told me very seriously that I should not lodge in that house, because shortly a dead (man's) coffin would be carried out of it, for (he saw) many were carrying of (and that was) when he was heard (to) cry.

I neglected his words and stayed there, (and) he said to others of the servants (that) he was sorry for it and that surely what he saw would shortly come to pass. (And) though no sick person was then there (in the house), yet the landlord, a healthy Highlander, died of an apoplectic fit before I left the house.

(Seer sees vision of soldiers eating barley)

In the year of 1653, Alexander Monro, afterwards Lieutenant Colonel to the Earl of Dumbarton's Regiment, and I, were walking in a place called Ullapool in Loch broom, on a little plain at the foot of a rugged hills. There was a servant working with a spade in the walk before us, (and) his back was to us, and his face to the hill. Before we came near to him he let the spade fall, and looked toward the hill; he (then) took notice of us as we passed near by him, which made me look at him, and perceiving him to stare a little strangely, I conjectured him to be a Seer. I called at (ie to) him, at which he started and smiled. What are you doing ? said I. He answered: I have seen a very strange thing, an army of Englishmen leading horses, coming down that hill, and a number of them eating the barley which is growing in the field near to the hill.

This was on the fourth of May, for I noted the day, and it was four or five weeks before the barley was sown in the field that he spoke of. Alexander Monro asked him how he knew they were Englishmen. He (the seer) said: because they were leading of horses, and had on hats and boots, which he knew no Scotsman would have there. We took little notice of the whole story as (anything) other than a foolish vision, but (we certainly) wished that an English party were there, we being then at war with them, and the place almost inaccessible for horsemen.

But in the middle of August thereafter, the Earl of Middleton, then Lieutenant for the King in the Highlands, having occasion to march a party of his towards the South Highlands, he sent his foot (soldiers) through a place called Inverlawel, and the fore-party which was first down the hill did fall of eating the barley which as on the little plain under it. Munro, calling to mind what the seer (had) told us in May preceding, he wrote of it, and sent an express (letter) to me in Loch Slin, in Ross, where I then was.

(Seer describes young lady's lover and husband-to-be)

I had occasion once to be in company where a young lady was, excuse my not naming of (actual) persons, and I was told there was a notable seer in the company. I called him to speak with me, as I did ordinarily when I found any of them, and after he had answered several questions, I asked if he knew any person to be in love with that (young) lady. He said (that) he did, but he knew not the person, for during the two days (that) he had been in her company, he perceived (some-)one standing near her, and his head (was) leaning on her shoulder, which, he said, did foretell that the man should marry her, and (then) die before her,a according to his observation.

This was in the year 1655. I desired him to describe the person (whom he saw), which he did, so that I could conjecture by the description of such a one (ie to be someone) who was (indeed) of that lady's acquaintance, though there were no thought of their marriage until two years after.

And having occasion in the year 1657 to find this seer who as an Islander in company with the other person whom I conjectured to have been described by him (in 1655), I called the seer aside and asked him if that was (indeed) the person (that) he saw beside the lady nearly two years past (as described above). The seer said it was he indeed, for he had seen that (same) lady just then, standing by him hand in hand. This (incident) was some few months before their marriage, and the man (whom the seer first described then subsequently met two years later) is since dead, and the lady (is) still alive (as the seer had predicted in 1655).

(Seer sees vision of dead man in chair next to Lord Tarbott, and is both right and wrong in his prediction)

I shall trouble you with but one more (example) which I thought (the) most remarkable of any that occurred to me. In January of 1652 the above mentioned Lieutenant Colonel Al. Monroe and I happened to be in the house of one William MacLeod of FerrinLea, in the country of Ross. Monroe, the Land Lord (ie MacLeod) and I were sitting in three chairs near the fire; in the corner of the great chimney were two Islanders, who had that very night come to the house, and were related to the Land Lord.

While one of these (islanders) was talking with Monroe, I perceived the other to look oddly toward me, (and) from his look, and his being an Islander, I conjectured him (to be) a seer, and asked him what he stared at? He answered by asking me to rise form the chair, for (he said) it was an unlucky one. I asked why, (and) he answered because there was a dead man in the chair next to me!

Well, said I, if he be in the next chair I may (therefore) keep my own, but what is the likeness of the (dead) man? The seer said he was a tall man with a long gray coat, booted, and one of his legs hanging over the arm of the chair, and his head hanging dead to the other side, and his arm backwards, as if it was broken.

There were some English troops quartered near that place, and there being at that time a great frost after a thaw, the country as covered all over with ice. Four or five of the English rode by this house (where we were staying), some two hours after the (seer's) vision, and while we were sitting by the fire we heard a great noise, which proved to be these troopers with the help of other servants, carrying in one of their number. He had taken a very mischievous fall, and had broken his arm, and was falling frequently into swooning fits. They brought him into the hall, and set him in the very chair and in the very posture that the seer had proposed (ie foreseen); but the man did not die, although he recovered with great difficulty.

(Seer predicts arrow wound, and seems to be mistaken)

Among the accounts given (to) me by Sir Normand Macleod there was one worthy of special notice, which was thus: there was a gentleman in the Isle of Harris, who was always seen by the seers with an arrow in his thigh. Such (of those dwelling) in the Isle who thought these prognostications infallible did not doubt but that he would be shot in the thigh before he died. Sir Norman told me that he heard it (to be) the subject of their discourse for many years, whenever that gentleman (with the visionary arrow in his thigh), was present.

At last the man died without any such accident, (and) Sir Norman was at his burial at Saint Clements Church in the (Isle of) Harris. At the same time the corpse of another gentleman was brought to be buried in the very same church. The friends on either die came to debate who should first enter the Church, ad in a trice from words they came to blows. One of the number who was armed with bow and arrows let fly (at) one (man) among them. Every family in that Isle have their burial place in the Church in a stone chest, and the bodies are carried in open biers to the burial place. Sir Norman, having appeased the tumult, found one of the arrows shot into the dead man's thigh. To this (event) Sir Norman himself was a witness.

(Girl with faery double described)

In the account which Mr Daniel Morrison, (a) parson in the (Isle of) Lewis gave me, there was one (event) which, though it may be heterogeneous from this subject (of the second sight), yet it may be worth your notice. It was of a young woman in his parish, who was mightily frightened by seeing own image, (standing) still before her, always when she came out into the open air. The back of the image being always to her, so that it was not a reflection as (might be seen) in a mirror, but the species (ie vision) of such a body as her own, and in a very like habit (ie clothing) which appeared to herself continually before her. The parson kept her a long while with him, but had no remedy of (ie for) her evil (ie ill) which troubled her exceedingly. I was told afterwards that when she was four or five years older, she saw it not (ie no longer).

(Possible causes of the Second Sight)

These are matters of fact which I assure you are truly related. But these and all others that occurred to me (ie which I encountered) by information or otherwise, could never lead me into a remote conjecture of the cause of so extraordinary a phenomenon. (I could not decide) whether it be a quality in the yes of some people in those parts, concurring with a quality in the air also. Whether such species (ie visions) be everywhere though not seen by (ie for) the want of eyes so qualified, or from whatever other cause, I must leave to enquiry of clearer judgement than mine. But a hint may be taken from this image which appeared (standing) still to the woman above mentioned, and from another mentioned by Aristotle in the fourth (book) of his Metaphysics, if I remember right, for it is (a) long (time) since I read it. And also from that common opinion that young infants, unsullied with many objects, do see apparitions which are not seen by those of elder years.

(Seers lose their abilities abroad)

Likewise from this, that several (of those that) did see (with) the second sight when in the highlands or Isles, when transported to live in other countries, especially in America, they quite lost this quality. This was told me by a gentleman who knew some of them in Barbados who did see no vision there, although he knew them to be seers when they lived in the Isles of Scotland.

Thus far My Lord Tarbott (Kirk's note: his commentary follows):

My Lord, after narrow inquisition has delivered many true and remarkable observes (observations) on this subject (of the second sight); yet to encourage further scrutiny I crave leave to say that:

1   But a few women are endowed with this (second) sight in respect of (ie by comparison to) men, and their predictions not so certain. (NOTE: Kirk says this in several places, yet he knew that women and men equally possessed Second Sight in the Highlands and Islands, and elsewhere describes a seeress calling up a powerful ally with a ritual. I suspect that he was protecting his own family, as he inherited the faery lore and healing powers from his mother, at a time when women were still being persecuted for witchcraft by the Puritans)

2   This sight is not criminal, since a man can come by it unawares, and without his consents, but its certain that he (will) see more fatal and fearful things than he (will) do gladsome.

3   The seers avouch that several (of those) who go to the Sith's (ie Sidh), or people at rest and in respect of us in (ie at) peace before the natural period of their life expires, do frequently appear unto them (ie to the seers).

(Faeries create or mime informative visions for the seers)

4   A vehement desire to attain this art (of the second sight) is very helpful to the inquirer, and the species (ie vision) of an absent friend, which appears to the seer as clearly as if he had sent his lively (ie living) picture to present itself before him, is no fantastic shadow of a sick apprehension, but a reality, and messenger coming for unknown reasons. (It comes) not from the original similitude of itself, but from a more swift and pragmatic people (ie the fairies), which (people) recreate themselves (ie entertain or find recreation) in offering secret intelligence to men, though generally they are unacquainted with that kind of correspondence, as if they lived in a different Element from them.

5   Though my collections were written long before I saw (those of) my Lord Tarbott's, yet I am glad that his descriptions and mine correspond so nearly (ie closely). The maid my Lord mentions who saw her image (standing) still before her suiteth (ie corresponds) with the Co-walker named in my (earlier) account. Which (Co-walker), some (people) at first thought might conjecture to be by the refraction of a cloud or mist as in the parallax, the whole air and every drop of water being a mirror to return the species (ie images) of things, were our visive faculties (ie our sight) sharp enough to apprehend them, or a natural reflection for the same reasons that an echo can be redoubled by air. Yet it were more feasible to impute this second sight to a quality infused into the eye by an unction; for witches have a sleeping ointment that when applied troubles their fantasy (ie imagination or dreaming), advancing it to have (within it) unusual figures and shapes, represented to it as if it were (in) a fit of fanaticism, hypochondriac melancholy, or possession of some insinuating spirit raising the soul beyond its common strain (ie level of existence).

(Causes of the Second Sight)

If the palpable instances and realities seen and innocently objected (ie shown) to the senses did not disprove it, and make this matter a palpable verity and no deception, (we might think it similar to the results of the witch's ointment), yet since this (second) sight can be bestowed without ointment or dangerous compact (ie pact), the qualification is not of so bad an original source (as that of witchcraft).

Therefore:

6   By my Lord (Tarbott's) good leave I presume to say that this (second) sight can be no quality of the air, nor of the eyes, because:

6,1: (they are people) such as live in the same air and see all other things as far off and as clearly, yet have not the second sight.

6,2: A seer can give another person this (second) sight transiently (ie temporarily) by putting his hand and foot in the posture he requires of him.

6,3: The unsullied eyes of infants can naturally perceive no new unaccustomed object but what (ie those which) appear to other men, unless exalted and clarified in some way as (in the Biblical example) of Balaam's ass for a time. Though in a witch's eye the beholder cannot see his own image reflected, as (he would) in the eyes of other people, so that (the) defect (ie absence) of objects as well as (the) diversity of the subject may operate differently on several (different) tempers (ie temperaments) and ages.

(Destructive power of the Sight in some people: See The Six Servants*)*

6,4: Though also some are of so venomous a constitution by being radicated (ie rooted) in envy and malice, that they pierce and kill, like a cockatrice, whatever creature they first set their eye on the morning. So was it with Walter Graham, sometime living in the same parish wherein now I am, who killed his own cow after commending its fatness, and shot a hare with his eye having praised its swiftness. Such was the infection of an (his) evil eye, albeit this was unusual; yet he saw no object but what(ever) was obvious to other men as well as to himself.

6,5: If the (fact of) being transported to live in another country did obscure the second sight, (then) neither the parson nor the maid (mentioned above) needed (to) be much troubled for (ie by) her (vision of a) reflex-self, as going from her wonted (ie usual) home (region) would have salved (ie healed) her fear.

Wherefore:

(Spiritual relationship between humans, faeries, and the Second Sight)

7: Since the things seen by the seers are real entities, the presages and predictions found true, (though) but a few (are) endowed with this (second) sight, and those (are) not (people) of bad lives or addicted to malefices (ie wrong doing), the true solution of the phenomenon seems rather to be (as follows). (They are the result of) the courteous endeavours of our fellow creatures in the invisible world to convince us, in opposition to Sadducees,

Socinians, and Atheists, of a Deity, (and) of Spirits, (and) of a possible and harmless method of correspondence betwixt men and them, even in this life. (And to convince us) of their operations for our caution and warning, (and) of the orders and degrees of Angels, whereof one order, with bodies of air condensed and curiously shaped, may be next to man (ie humankind), superior to him in understanding, yet unconfirmed; and of their region (of) habitation and influences on man, greater than that of the stars upon inanimate bodies. A knowledge reserved for these last atheistic ages, wherein the profanity of men's lives has debauched and blinded their understandings as to Moses, Jesus, and the prophets, unless they get (such) convictions from things formerly known, as from the Regions of the Dead.

(Loss and recovery of Second Sight in foreign lands)
Nor does the ceasing of the visions, upon the seer's transmigration into foreign kingdoms make his Lordship's conjecture of the quality of the air and eye (as above) a whit more probable. On the contrary, it confirms greatly my account of an invisible people, guardian over and careful of (the welfare of) men. (Those fairy people) have their different offices (ie roles) and abilities in distant countries as appears in Daniel 10.13 etc. about Israel's, Greece's, and Persia's assistant princes, whereof who so (of the assistant princes) prevails gives dominion and ascendancy to his pupils (ie peoples) and vassals, over the opposite armies and countries. So (it is) that every country and kingdom having their topical (ie local) spirits or powers assisting and governing them, (then) the Scottish seer banished to America, being a stranger there as well (ie as much) to the invisible as to the visible inhabitants, and wanting (ie lacking) the familiarity of his former correspondents, he could not have the favour and warnings, (given) by the several visions and predictions, which were once granted (to) him by those acquaintances and favourites in his own country.

For if what he (the seer was used) to see were realities, as I have made (clear evidence) appear (ie prove), it were to great an honour for Scotland to have such seldom-seen Watchers and predominant powers over it alone, acting in it so expressly, and (leaving) all other nations wholly destitute of the like. Though (it might be said), without all peradventure (ie without being too risky), (that) all other people(s) wanted (ie lacked) the right key of their Cabinet, and (lacked) the exact method of correspondence with them (ie the fairies), except (for) the sagacious active Scots, a (great) many of whom have retained it (ie the second sight) for a long time, and by surprises and Raptures do often foretell what, in kindness, is really (ie truly) represented to them at several occasions.
Here our quotes on faery beings and the Second Sight from Kirk and Tarbott finish.

Afterword

The Future

What of the future? With each artificial or calculated millennium human cultures feel that radical changes will come...such changes are mainly observed in retrospect. The true cycles, which we approach through arts such as astrology or sciences such as physics, are connected to relativity, the relationship between our planet, our sun, our solar system. Beyond this are the universal connections, those of our solar system to other stars as they move through time and space. The idea of such cycles is also found in the faery tradition, though there is no strict or well-defined information or chronology handed down.

In astrology the relationships that imply cycles of change are identified by an artificial model, calculated against an idealised backdrop of the Zodiac. Curiously, it often works with great accuracy. In mythology, we find that universal relationships, and their changes or interactions resonating through human consciousness, are embodied as deities, as legends, and as visions of creation and apocalypse. Sometimes the mythic themes contain symbols or images from earlier astrological models, as with the legends of the Titans in Greek myth, who begin as planetary powers, but become Underworld powers with the arrival of the Olympian deities.

The theme of an old divine order of beings cycling from the stellar realms into the Earth or local planetary body is found in myth and religion worldwide, and reveals profound insights into what seem to us to be long term cycles of transformation within the holism of our planet. It is at this profound level that the faery tradition holds knowledge of planetary changes, with the more powerful allies and Sleepers involved in long-term climate and weather patterns, geomantic and seismic movements and so forth.

In the faery tradition there are several such strands referring to the greater picture, that of the life cycle of the land, the planet within the living and moving solar system, and the universal creation and apocalypse. The life of the land (any land) is embodied in the local or racial mythology as verses or stories about successive arrivals or appearances, a typical example being the Irish *Book of Invasions*, or the medieval *History of the British Kings*, both books formalised into text from oral tradition.

The theme of successive races or waves of beings and their interaction is found in all mythologies, and is closely linked to transformations of the land itself, for each wave of appearances of beings modifies the land. This local or ethnic stream of myth is linked to the ideas of cosmic creation, for they are octaves or resonances of one another, and are often difficult to separate in an analytic manner. The overall idea is that the universe is mirrored in the particular. In mysticism, in metaphysics, we find the idea that a human mirrors the divine, that the entire universe of beings is found in one part, a typical theme of holism. In myth and legend we find that localities, lands, and zones, all mirror the life of the planet, and simultaneously that of the solar system and universe. They are part of one another, and so they ceaselessly interact.

When you read this book again, try beginning with the last chapter, and read it in reverse order towards the Foreword. It is, after all, a book about the living world of faery, which is a mirror image of our own in which time flows differently and space is often irrelevant. Like many faery subjects, the book has been arranged so that it can be read forwards then backwards. Try it.

If you have completed this ramble through the faery realm, you will have found many signposts for further exploration. The faery realm is one of our major ways towards, and sources of, transformation, long neglected, but still potent. The transformation is of ourselves, our land, our planet. It is your adventure: enter into it, and transform.

Booklist

NOTE : For guided visualisation and music cassettes on the Faery and Underworld traditions written and performed by R J Stewart, please write to Sulis Music, BCM 3721, London, WC1N 3XX.

(1)   Robert Kirk, *Walker Between Worlds* a new edition of *The Secret Commonwealth* in modern English with commentary: R J Stewart, Element Books 1991
The Secret Commonwealth edited A Lang, David Nutt, London, 1893.
The Secret Commonwealth edited S Sanderson. Folklore Society, Mistletoe Series. Other references to the Second Sight and Faery tradition are found in:
Folklore of the Scottish Highlands A Ross, Batsford, London, 1976.
Pagan Celtic Britain, A Ross, Cardinal, 1974.
A Collection of Highland Rites and Customes ed. J L Campbell, Folklore Society, Cambridge, 1975.
A Description of the Western Islands of Scotland M Martin. Published London, 1703. Republished Eneas Mackay, Stirling, 1934.
Dueteroscopia Rev. John Fraser, Symson, Edinburgh 1707.
A Journey to the Western Islands of Scotland Samuel Johnson, Strahan and Cadell, London, 1775.
Witchcraft and Second Sight in the Highlands and Islands of Scotland, J G Campbell, Glasgow, 1902.
Sketches descriptive of Picturesque Scenery on the Southern Confines of Perthshire P Graham, 1806 & 1812.
Samuel Pepys: (Vol. 3) The Saviour of the Navy Arthur Bryant, Collins, London, 1938.
John Dee, Charlotte Fell Smith, Constable & Co, London, 1909.
The Heptarchia Mystica of John Dee, edited Robert Turner, No. 17, Hermetic Opus Sourceworks Series, Edinburgh, 1983.
John Dee, The Elizabethan Merlin Gareth Knight in Merlin and Woman ed. R J Stewart, Blandford Press, London, 1988.
Elements of Prophecy R J Stewart, Elements Books, Shaftesbury, 1990.

Carmina Gadelica edited Alexander Carmichael, 5 Volumes, Edinburgh.

(2) *The Teachings of Don Juan* and subsequent titles by Carlos Castenada, published by Simon and Schuster USA, and Century UK.

(3) *The Fairy Faith in Celtic Countries* W Y Evans Wentz, Oxford University Press, 1911. New edition with Foreword by Kathleen Raine, Colin Smythe Ltd, Gerrards Cross, England. Humanities Press, Atlantic Highlands, New Jersey, USA, 1977.

(4) *The Tibetan Book of the Dead* edited by W Y Evans Wentz, various editions.

(5) *The Types of the Folktale*, A Aarne, trans. & enlarged by Stith Thompson, Folklore Fellows Communications No 184, Helsinki, 1961.

(6) *The UnderWorld Initiation* R J Stewart, Aquarian Press, Wellingborough, 1986 & 1989. Also:
Earthlight R J Stewart, Element Books, Shaftesbury, 1992.
and *Power within the Land*, Element Books, Shaftesbury, 1993.

(7) *The Fairy Tale Reader* edited J & C Matthews, Aquarian Press, London, 1993; quotes Spence. This source book is highly recommended. Also:
The Fairy Tradition in Britain L Spence, Rider & Co, London, 1948 and other titles by the same author.

(8) *The Celtic Twilight* W B Yeats, Lawrence and Bullen, London, 1893.
Irish Fairy and Folk Tales W B Yeats, Walter Scott, London, 1893.

(9) *The Immortal Hour* Fiona Macleod (William Sharp) in Vol VII Collected Works, William Heinemann Ltd, London, 1933. *The Immortal Hour* (Opera) by Rutland Boughton (with libretto) Hyperion Records, London (new digital recording, 1987).

(10) *A Dictionary of Fairies* Katherine Briggs, Alan Lane, 1976.

(11) *The Candle of Vision* A E (George William Russell). First published 1918, then by Quest Books, USA, 1974.

(12) *Puck of Pook's Hill* Rudyard Kipling, various editions.

(14) *The Ladder of Lights* Helios Books, Toddington, 1968. Also: *Magical Ritual Methods* Helios Books, Toddington, 1969. See also my own books for subsequent development of the tradition: *Living Magical Arts* R J Stewart, Blandford Press, Poole, 1987. *Advanced Magical Arts* R J Stewart, Element Books, Shaftesbury, 1988.

(15) *Legendary Britain* John Matthews and R J Stewart, Blandford Press, London, 1989.

(16) *The Dreampower Tarot Deck and Book* by R J Stewart, paintings by Stuart Littlejohn. Aquarian Press (Harper Collins) London, 1993.

(17) *The Stars and the Stones* M Brennan, Thames and Hudson, London, 1983.
Megalithic Sites in Britain A Thom, Oxford, 1967.

Megalithic Lunar Observatories A Thom, Oxford, 1971.

(18) *The Gospel of the Essenes* edited and translated by E B Szekely. C W Daniel Co Ltd, London, 1976. Also:

The Gnostic Gospels E Pagels, Weidenfeld and Nicolson Ltd, London, 1979.

(19) *Meditation and Kabbalah* Aryeh Kaplan, Weiser, USA, 1985.

(20) *Celtic Gods and goddesses* R J Stewart, Blandford Press, London, 1990 and the companion volume:

Celtic Myths, Celtic Legends Blandford Press, 1994. See also:

Celtic Heritage A & B Rees, Thames and Hudson, London,1974.

Elements of Creation Myth R J Stewart, Element Books, Shaftesbury, 1989.

Gothic Image Tours

We organize 10- and 14-day tours to the ancient sacred sites of Britain and Ireland. These journeys are accompanied by authors and researchers including the author of this volume, Bob Stewart.

If you would like to receive a brochure, please contact:

Jamie George
Gothic Image Tours
7 High Street
Glastonbury
Somerset
England   BA6 9DP

Telephone: 01458 831453
Fax:: 01458 831666

Index

Tarbott, Lord 198, 201, 203–206
  relations 198
  report 198
Titans x
  in Greek myth 208
Tradition 11, 80, 188
Tree 15, 23, 177
  the Inverted 115
  the sacred Apple 91
Tree of Life 78, 79

U

Underworld ix, 15, xix, 21–23, 73, 80, 87, 89, 98–101, 103, 105, 113, 116, 163–164, 167
  and faery 91
  contact 105
  dimensions 163
  energies 98

  experience 91
  initiations 47
  paths and gates 104
  powers 208
  realms 103
  techniques 100
  tradition 40–41, 47, 51, 163
USA ix

V

Virginia, seers in 5, 66, 69
Voices 163, 166
Voices of Many 163, 165–166

W

Well 170, 171
Wentz Evans 2, 7, 16–17, xxi, 33, 45, 60, 111, 130, 152, 157, 174

Gothic Image Tours

We organize 10- and 14-day tours to the ancient sacred sites of Britain and Ireland. These journeys are accompanied by authors and researchers including the author of this volume, Bob Stewart.

If you would like to receive a brochure, please contact:

Jamie George
Gothic Image Tours
7 High Street
Glastonbury
Somerset
England   BA6 9DP

Telephone: 01458 831453
Fax: 01458 831666